# THE ABCs OF
# QUILTMAKING

## Piecing, Appliqué, Quilting & More

*Janet Lundholm McWorkman*

**C&T** PUBLISHING

**Publisher:** Amy Marson

**Creative Director:** Gailen Runge

**Editor:** Monica Gyulai

**Technical Editor:** Debbie Rodgers

**Cover Designer:** Page + Pixel

**Book Designer:** Kristen Yenche

**Production Coordinator / Illustrator:** Tim Manibusan

**Production Editor:** Alice Mace Nakanishi

**Photo Assistant:** Carly Marin

**Photography** by Diane Pedersen of C&T Publishing, unless otherwise noted

Library of Congress Cataloging-in-Publication Data

Names: McWorkman, Janet Lundholm, 1953- author.

Title: The ABCs of quiltmaking : piecing, appliqué, quilting & more / Janet Lundholm McWorkman.

Description: Lafayette, California : C&T Publishing, Inc., 2016.

Identifiers: LCCN 2016004337 | ISBN 9781617452222 (soft cover)

Subjects: LCSH: Quilting--Patterns. | Patchwork--Patterns. | Appliqué--Patterns.

Classification: LCC TT835 .M4785 2016 | DDC 746.46--dc23

LC record available at http://lccn.loc.gov/2016004337

Printed in China

10 9 8 7 6 5 4 3 2 1

## Acknowledgments

I had an enormous amount of help writing and sewing for this book. Marcia Harmening sent a photo of *The Quilter's Primer* to C&T Publishing acquisitions editor, Roxanne Cerda. Roxanne then helped me put the book into outline form. And editors Monica Gyulai and Debbie Rodgers beat the book into submission.

Lisa Bauer, Marcia Harmening, Dana Hyams, Jane Olsen, Heidi Uselmann, Terri Wangstrom, and Pam Wicks all sewed quilt projects for *The Quilter's Primer*. Aurifil Threads, Moda, and Quilter's Dream Cotton supplied thread, fabric, and batting for the quilts.

And lastly, my lovely husband, Don, always knew I could do it, even when I didn't.

Many tips and tricks come courtesy of The Italy Ladies—
*Back row:* Heidi Uselmann, Janet McWorkman, Lisa Bauer (*in white*), Dana Hyams, Jane Olsen;
*Front row:* Terri Wangstrom (*in green*), Marcia Harmening

# CONTENTS

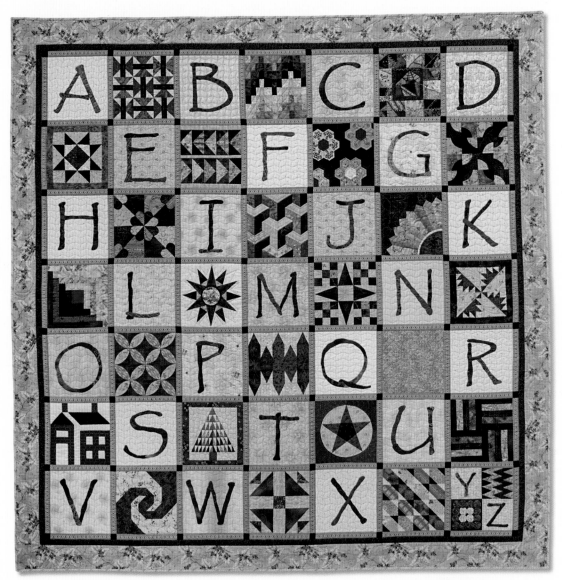

*The Quilter's Primer*, 88″ × 88″, designed and pieced by Janet McWorkman, quilted by Linda Weaver

*The ABCs of Quiltmaking* takes its cues from an old-fashioned school primer. It's designed to be used in order, like a workbook.

First, learn about the tools, terms, and techniques that are the bedrock of quiltmaking. Expect to refer back to these early chapters often, especially the techniques taught in Quiltmaking Basics (page 13). If you come upon a term you don't know, check the Glossary (page 7) for a definition. And when a particular ruler, glue, or other product is recommended for a technique and you need to know more, turn to Tools of the Trade (page 6).

When you are ready to begin sewing, start with the first, most basic blocks. As you work your way through the book, the blocks will get more complicated, building on the skills you've already learned. Many chapters include Key Techniques that you will use again and again. Think of *The ABCs of Quiltmaking* like taking a course. You will be a very versatile quilter when you graduate!

Don't forget that you have the world at your fingertips. Look online for tutorials demonstrating the techniques explained in the book. Sometimes a video is worth a thousand words.

Each chapter has a few blocks that share construction techniques and most include a project or two based on just those blocks. Make a wallhanging or a set of place mats as you build skills.

If you stick with the book from start to finish, you also will be able to make a sampler—your own version of *The Quilter's Primer* (page 4), an alphabet quilt that requires as many different quilting skills as could gracefully fit into a single quilt. This teaching tool is designed to take you on a journey into the craft of quiltmaking that contains every block in the quilt, plus blocks appliquéd with the whole alphabet.

Have patience and take the time to learn the skills needed to make your own primer and you will have the skills to elevate this craft into art. I applaud anyone who starts on a crafting journey, knowing they'll make mistakes. Some skills may take a few tries. But if you work through this book in order, you will get the experience and confidence you need to move to more difficult blocks.

# MAKE A QUILTER'S PRIMER

This materials list allows you to plan your whole quilt from start to finish. However, you can also make blocks as you go and let random color combinations emerge, instead of planning out your whole design before you begin. If you want to design as you go, then you will probably purchase additional small cuts of fabric as you make more blocks and develop a sense of the design of your sampler.

## Materials

**Focal fabric:** 2–3 yards, depending on how much you love it

**Pieced blocks:** Start with 8–10, but eventually you will need closer to 20 quarter-yard cuts (These can be fat quarters.)

**Background of appliqué letters:** 3 yards

**Appliqué letters:** 1¼ yards of a single fabric or 1¾ yards of a variety of fabrics

**Sashing:** 1½ yards

**Inner border:** ½ yard

**Outer border:** 1½ yards

**Cornerstones:** ¼ yard

**Binding:** 1 yard

**Backing:** 7¾ yards

**Batting:** 92″ × 92″ (king size)

The finished size of each block in *The Quilter's Primer* is 10″ × 10″. Each block has a materials list that notes the minimum size of the fabric pieces needed to make the block. You do not need to cut a piece of fabric to this size before cutting the individual pieces for the block construction.

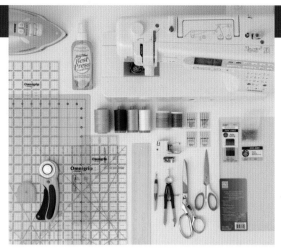

# GETTING STARTED

## TOOLS OF THE TRADE

Quilters collect tools, gadgets, and widgets. Every craft and quilt shop has hundreds of items to assist the quilter, from simple scissors to complex specialty machines. Listed in this chapter are the tools I can't quilt without. I promise I won't ask you to purchase items you won't use! When shopping for quilting tools, try them out, if possible.

| TOOL | DETAILS | MY PREFERRED BRANDS |
|---|---|---|
| Sewing machine in good working order | If you have a sewing machine, it will most likely be adequate for learning how to quilt. You will need two specialty feet, listed below. | If you have to purchase a sewing machine, test several, check online reviews, and talk to friends for recommendations. I use a Janome Jem Platinum and a Brother PQ1500. |
| ¼˝ foot | Specialty foot for your sewing machine | Check which brand will work with your machine. |
| Walking foot | Specialty foot for your sewing machine | Check which brand will work with your machine. |
| Rotary cutter and blades | 45 mm | Olfa or Fiskars |
| Self-healing mat | 24˝ × 36˝ | Olfa or Fiskars |
| Rotary ruler | 6˝ × 24˝ and 4˝ × 12˝ | Omnigrid or Creative Grids |
| Square ruler | 10½˝ × 10½˝ | Omnigrid or Creative Grids |
| Add-A-Quarter ruler | 6˝ yellow | CM Designs |
| Fabric scissors | Titanium, microtip | Fiskars or Gingher (Label these "FABRIC ONLY.") |
| Paper scissors | Any old scissors will work | Label these "PAPER ONLY." |
| Piecing thread | 100% cotton at 40–50 weight | Aurifil and Güttermann are good choices. |
| Quilting thread | Cotton or cotton/poly blends | In addition to the brands above, Sulky, Superior, and YLI have interesting threads. |
| Pins | Glass head, extra long | Dritz or Clover |
| Sewing machine needles | 80/12 and 90/14 | Schmetz brand is my first choice. Finer needles are used for piecing; thicker needles are used for machine quilting. |
| Hand sewing needles | Sizes 6–10 (or whatever is most comfortable to use) | John James brand is my favorite. Just be sure you can see the eye to thread it! |
| School compass | Needed to draw circles at least 11˝ in diameter | Any inexpensive compass will do the trick. |
| Seam ripper | A necessary evil | Dritz or Clover |
| Template sheets | Heat-resistant sheets, 6 sheets per package | Templar |
| Iron and spray bottles for water and starch | The iron you own will probably be fine. A higher wattage works better. | Any major brand name with 1400+ watts will work. I have a Shark and a Rowenta. |
| Starch | Liquid starch for appliqué | I like Mary Ellen's Best Press or any liquid starch. |

Find a box or plastic tub to store all your quilting tools. Label each tool with your initials where possible. Your tools represent a fairly sizable investment and will give you years of service if treated well.

*tip*

A rotary cutter is an extremely useful and dangerous tool. Keep it away from children. Make a habit of closing it after each use. Seriously … *Close it after each use!*

# GLOSSARY

Quilting has a language all its own. Knowing the lingo will not only help you understand this book but will also engage you with the entire quilting community. Please review the glossary of quilting terms—a fat quarter is not a district in New Orleans. Learn the basic definitions and refer back to them as you progress through *The ABCs of Quiltmaking*.

**Appliqué**   Sewing fabric pieces to a larger background, typically curved pieces. This can be done by machine, by hand, or with fusible web products.

**Backing**   The fabric used for the back of a quilt.

**Bargello**   A technique of sewing together many strips of fabric, subcutting these strips, and then arranging them in vertical columns to create undulating waves.

**Basting stitch**   A long stitch used for stabilizing edges or holding together two fabrics. It is generally temporary and is often, but not always, removed.

**Batik**   A method of dying fabric that involves wax resist or glue to prevent dye from coloring designed areas.

**Batting**   The middle layer of a quilt; provides depth and warmth.

**Bearding**   The action of batting coming through to the front or back fabric of a quilt, creating undesirable fuzzy spots.

**Bias**   The 45° diagonal between the fabric's cross grain and its selvage.

**Binding**   Thin strips of fabric, often doubled, used to finish the outside edges of a quilt.

**Chain piecing**   Sewing together fabric units without removing each individual unit from the sewing machine before moving to the next seam.

**Cornerstones**   Squares of fabric placed at the corners of blocks between sashing strips.

**Crazy quilt**   A piecing technique that involves improvisation instead of a pattern.

**Cross grain of fabric**   The direction of grain or weave running from selvage to selvage. This is also referred to as *weft*.

**Dog-ears**   Points of fabric extending beyond the seam allowance that occur when piecing diagonals.

**Fat quarter**   A quarter-yard of fabric subcut widthwise from a half-yard piece, resulting in a piece measuring approximately 18″ × 22″.

**Feed dogs**   The mechanical teeth on the bed of a sewing machine that assist with the fabric's forward movement as you sew. These are dropped or covered for free-motion quilting.

**Finger-pressing**   Running a fingernail over the seam rather than pressing with an iron.

**Flimsy**   The unquilted top ready to be sandwiched. This is often referred to as the top.

**Foundation piecing**   A method of piecing by sewing directly on a foundation of muslin or plain fabric, adding stability. Foundation piecing is often used when piecing Crazy Quilt blocks.

**Focal fabric**   The fabric that sets the tone for the quilt. Generally, a multicolored large-scale print that is often repeated in blocks and borders.

**Free-motion quilting**   The action of quilting with the feed dogs dropped without the aid of a stitching pattern.

**Fusible web**   A material with a thin layer of heat-activated glue used to fuse together two fabrics. Often used with appliqué.

**Half-square triangle**   A square formed by sewing together two fabric squares along the diagonal.

**Hanging sleeve**   A tube of fabric sewn to the back of a quilt, enabling the quilt to be hung on a wall.

**Improvisational piecing**   Piecing without the use of a specific pattern; instead, quilters choose the fabric and shape of the piece as they sew.

**Length of grain**   The direction of grain or weave running parallel to the selvage. This is also referred to as *warp*.

**Loft**   The depth of batting material.

**Longarm**   A special kind of sewing machine used to machine quilt. The patterns can be computer generated or hand guided. A longarm quilter is a person who uses such a machine and is often available for hire.

**Low volume**   Fabrics that "read" as lights and often have secondary patterns or design elements. Can also be light, neutral solids.

**Mitered corners**   Forming a neat corner on the diagonal with either a border or a binding.

**Paper piecing**   A method of piecing where a pattern is drawn on paper and the fabric is then stitched directly on the paper. This method allows for very precise, intricate piecing.

**Piecing**   Sewing together smaller pieces of fabric into larger units, forming a quilt top.

**Primer**   A beginner's manual, as in *The Dick and Jane Primer*, published in the 1930s; pronounced with a short *i*.

**Quarter-inch quilting foot**   A sewing machine attachment that guides fabric at a precise ¼″ seam allowance.

**Quarter-square triangle**   A pieced square made of two or three fabrics sewn together along their diagonals.

**Rotary cutter**   A circular cutting tool (similar to a pizza cutter) that is used with a self-healing mat and rotary rulers to cut fabric. It is a seriously sharp tool and should be used carefully.

**Sandwich**   The three layers of a quilt: top, batting, and backing.

**Sashing**   Strips of fabric sewn between pieced blocks that enlarge the overall quilt and add a new design element.

**Scale**   The relative size of a print or plaid, as in small or large scale.

**Scant quarter inch**   A tiny bit less than a quarter inch.

**Seam allowance**   The width of a sewn seam. Quilters adhere to a strict, scant quarter-inch seam allowance.

**Self-healing mat**   The cutting surface used with a rotary cutter. It is soft so that it doesn't damage the blade, yet thick enough to protect the work surface.

**Selvage**   The lengthwise edges of fabric, finished so they don't unravel.

**Set-in seam**   A seam that progresses along a different diagonal than the straight seam leading to it.

**Square-up**   Trimming the edges of a block or a quilt top to ensure square corners.

**Stash**   A quilter's personal collection of fabric (which seems to grow of its own volition!).

**Subcut**   To cut smaller pieces of fabric from a piece previously cut.

**Template**   A fixed pattern that can be used repeatedly by either cutting or tracing around it.

**Top**   A finished quilt top ready to be sandwiched and quilted, sometimes called a *flimsy*.

**Unfinished projects (UFOs)**   A collection of quilt projects in various stages of completion. The longer you quilt, the more UFOs you'll have.

**Value**   The relative darkness or lightness of a color.

**Width of fabric (WOF)**   The cutting direction across the cross grain (or weft) of fabric, from selvage to selvage (often 40″–45″).

**Yo-yos**   A circle of fabric gathered up like a small purse and ironed flat. Generally made with small scraps of fabric, Yo-yo quilts do not have batting or backing and are often called summer quilts.

# FABRIC

Quilting is all about fabric. Ask quilters what whets their enthusiasm, and I bet they'll say fabric. If possible, find a local shop, get a buddy, and go fondle the fabric. Look at solids, prints, stripes, and themed fabrics. Stretch your fabric acumen by taking a picture of a favorite quilt and trying to find similar fabrics. Learn the layout of the shop. Ask questions of the shop staff. You'll be spending time in your local quilt shop, so you'll want to know where things are. Often shops have loyalty programs for discounts. They may also offer classes or have bulletin boards where quilting events are advertised.

Use 100 percent midweight cotton for quilts. Your local quilt shop will carry hundreds of choices of good-quality cotton fabric. Don't be tempted by cotton/poly blends. They may be cheaper, but they also act differently when sewn, ironed, stretched, quilted, and washed.

If you don't have a local quilt shop, the Resources (page 79) lists many online suppliers.

When selecting fabric for a quilt, some guidelines will serve you well. As you gain color confidence, branch out from these tried-and-true methods to find your own color style.

## Guidelines

### 1. CHOOSE ONE FABRIC YOU LOVE AS YOUR FOCAL FABRIC.

A focal fabric should have at least three colors. It is usually not a plaid or a stripe. It often is a large-scale print.

Daiwabo focal fabric

### 2. CHOOSE ADDITIONAL FABRICS THAT PLAY WELL WITH YOUR FOCAL FABRIC.

Place your choices together to see if any should be eliminated. Are there too many lights? Are there too many solids?

Focal fabric for *The Quilter's Primer* with many coordinating fabrics

Focal fabric with twelve coordinating fabrics

### 3. CHOOSE FABRICS THAT HAVE SOME CONTRAST AND INTEREST.

The addition of colors can add contrast and interest, which can also be achieved by varying the relative brightness or darkness of coordinating fabrics. This is called color value. If all your fabrics are pale pink, why cut them up and sew them together again? You want to be able to see your fabrics as individuals as well as friends. The fabric selection for a nicely balanced quilt will use several values.

Focal fabric with additional colors added

## 4. CHOOSE FABRICS THAT HAVE A VARIETY OF PRINT SCALE.

The scale of the fabric refers to the size of the print. A very large-scale print, while great for a focal fabric, may not work as well as a coordinating fabric. Large-scale prints lose their effect when cut up into small pieces. Solids, small and medium prints, stripes, and plaids all have possibilities as coordinating fabrics.

Elephant print with coordinating palette in a variety of scale

Navy palette with a variety of scale

## 5. CHOOSE A LIMITED NUMBER OF PRIMARY COLORS.

All three primary colors used in one piece can look cartoonish. Imagine the blue, yellow, and red of Superman's logo. It isn't impossible to use all the primary colors successfully, but it's difficult to balance. In the Moda example, the focal fabric has all primary colors represented. However, the coordinating fabrics deemphasize the blue and yellow to focus on the secondary colors of green and orange.

Moda fabric palette with limited primary colors

*tip*

Want to learn more about color? Craftsy.com has excellent free color tutorials. The Ultimate 3-in-1 Color Tool by Joen Wolfrom (from C&T Publishing) is an invaluable reference to boost your color knowledge. Or head to your local library or used bookstore for books on color theory.

Ultimate 3-in-1 Color Tool

## Tutorial: Selecting Fabric for a Quilt

Choosing fabric for a quilt is a process. Here are some tips and a one-page visual tutorial to walk you through some choices.

*tip*

If choosing fabric combinations makes you uncomfortable, duplicate the colors in a favorite quilt or photo. The exercise of matching fabric colors, values, and print scale will boost your confidence. Besides, imitation is the highest form of flattery!

*tip*

Take your most beloved fabric and study it well. What percentage is represented by each color? What values are the colors? Is it 80 percent light, neutral fabric with a pop of brightness? Then base your quilt on that fabric by selecting mostly low-volume fabrics with only a few brights. Is it a historic reproduction fabric? If so, a variety of small-scale prints will coordinate well.

When selecting a focal fabric for quilt, consider the fabric's color percentages. If you love a fabric that has a predominance of one color, it may be more pleasing to reproduce those percentages in a quilt featuring that fabric.

Gray flags focal fabric with equal percentages of colors represented

Color percentages altered to reflect the focal fabric

Finding a palette that works is a process. Start by auditioning candidates.

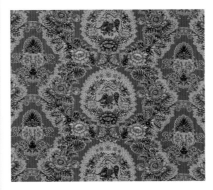

A beautiful historic reproduction can be used as a focal fabric and presents several possible color directions.

Too many primary colors

An interesting monochromatic red palette

Pretty busy

Civil War fabric final cut

Philip Jacobs blue petunias focal fabric

Represented colors

Final cut

Juvenile trucks as focal fabric

Starting out

Final cut

## Preparing Fabric for a Quilt

There are many different opinions about how to prepare fabric to use in a quilt. The cardinal rule is to treat all the fabrics used in one project the same way.

I suggest, at a minimum, to wash, dry, and lightly press all your fabric. This way, you won't risk ruining a finished quilt with a color that bleeds when it's first washed. Most quilt-shop quality cottons are very color stable, but there are always exceptions. Wash dark and light fabrics separately. Products such as Retayne color fixative and Shout Color Catchers can reduce the chance of a fabric losing its color and ruining other fabrics in the load.

Another good reason to prewash fabric is that cotton shrinks. Wash and dry your fabrics before sewing them into quilts so they don't shrink after you are done.

Cotton batik fabrics are saturated with color and bleed more than other printed cottons. Wash and dry them before using them in a quilt.

Retayne, Orvus Quilt Soap, and Shout Color Catchers

I am often asked how I manage a growing stash of fabric. I sort fabric first by essential type of fabric, such as loosely woven cotton, batik, flannel, or cotton/linen blend. Then I sort by color. Find a system that works for you. When starting a fabric collection, a couple shelves or a few clear plastic buckets will work fine.

Protect your stash from the elements. Avoid fading and mold by keeping your fabric out of airtight containers and away from direct sunlight.

# DESIGN WALL

And finally, before you get into building beautiful blocks, you may want to create a design wall. It is a great thing. It isn't essential, but it doesn't take much money and is invaluable when organizing finished quilt blocks.

The simplest design wall can be made from an inexpensive vinyl, flannel-backed tablecloth. Tack it to a wall, tape it to a closet door, or simply place it on the floor. Organized blocks can be rolled up in the tablecloth for storage or left up to admire. With a bit more effort, you can use three 1″-thick, 3 × 8–foot insulation sheets (available at home improvement big box stores) and a queen-size quilt batt to make a giant, permanent design wall.

There's a great tutorial on making an inexpensive design wall on the Happy Stash Quilts website: happystashquilts.com > Blog > January 20, 2015: "Make a Design Wall for About $50— As Easy as 1, 2, 3."

## ROTARY CUTTING

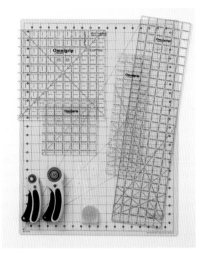

Rotary cutting tools

Mastering the use of a rotary cutter is the first skill you need. To start, gather scrap fabric, a cutter, a self-healing mat, and an acrylic ruler. Practice on scraps of fabric until you feel confident enough to tackle more expensive fabric.

### *tip*

The rotary cutter, invented in 1979 by Olfa founder, Yoshio Okada, changed how quilters cut fabric. Until then, precision cutting required cardboard templates—and a prayer.

**1.** Fold your fabric selvage to selvage and adjust the edges until the fabric hangs straight, without any diagonal folds. Place the folded edge on your cutting mat, with the fold of the fabric on a horizontal straight line.

**2.** Place your 6″ × 24″ ruler on the fabric, aligning it with a vertical inch mark on the mat.

**3.** With the rotary cutter placed against the right side of the ruler, slice up the right side of the fabric. (Reverse this procedure if you're left-handed.) Push the rotary cutter next to the ruler's edge upward and *away from all your body parts*. Practice subcutting smaller pieces by rotating the strips 90° and repeating the cutting procedure.

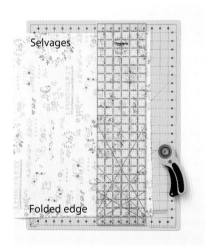

Line up the rough right edge of the fabric. (Reverse this procedure if you are left-handed.)

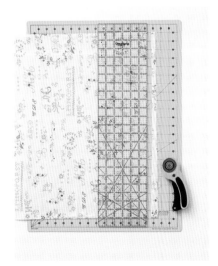

Trim away the rough edge.

Cut strips using the ruler and mat lines.

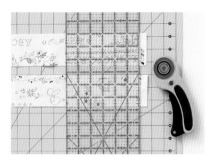

Trim selvage edges from the right side of the strips.

*tip*

If your ruler slides around, stick small circles of adhesive-backed sandpaper to the underside to make it grip better.

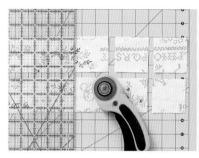

Subcut strips to make perfect squares.

## SEWING BLOCKS

### Precise Seam Allowances

When you sew together pieces of fabric for a quilt block, it's really important to sew a precise distance from the edge. In quilting, that distance—called a seam allowance—is ¼″.

Practice getting it right on scraps and then measure afterward to check your accuracy.

If you think I'm being too fussy, just do the math. If there are twenty seams across the width of your quilt top and each seam is off by only ¹⁄₁₆″, that will add up to a 2½″ error. That's a big deal. But practice will eliminate the problem.

**1.** Rotary cut a piece of scrap fabric 20″ × 1½″.

**2.** Subcut this strip into 4 pieces, each 4½″ × 1½″. Select a neutral thread color that works well with most of the fabric in your project. You don't need to match each fabric exactly. A neutral tone that blends will work well.

**3.** Sew together the 4 strips and press the seams to one side. Measure your finished square. It should measure exactly 4½″ × 4½″. If it is wider, your seam allowance is too narrow. If it is not wide enough, your seam allowance is too fat. Repeat this exercise until you are happy with the results.

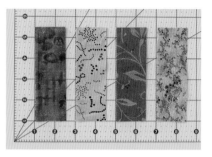

¼″ seam practice

Finished ¼″ test square

*tip*

All sewing machines are not created equal. If you change midproject to a different machine, repeat the seam allowance practice piece to identify the exact ¼″ seam location.

### Stitch Length

■ For general piecing, use a stitch length of about 14–18 stitches per inch with cotton.

■ When paper piecing, reduce your stitch length to 24 stitches (or more) per inch. This will perforate the paper and make it easier to remove.

■ A stitch length of 10 stitches per inch is used to stabilize the edges of a quilt before sewing the layers together.

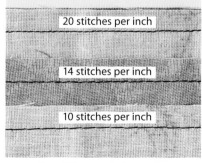

20 stitches per inch

14 stitches per inch

10 stitches per inch

Use different stitch lengths for different purposes.

# Chain Piecing

Speed up your quiltmaking and waste less thread by chain piecing. Instead of sewing together quilt units one at a time, prepare a stack of them and sew them together one after the other, without stopping each time you finish one. It's faster and more fun.

Sew together many pairs of fabric pieces without stopping, forming a chain.

Snip thread only after sewing together many units.

Chain piece again to add another fabric.

# Matching Seams

Take time to sew and press seams neatly and accurately so that they come together perfectly when joined with other pieced units. If you're off by a thread or two, don't sweat it. After all, quilting isn't about being perfect. But if you're off by more, it's best to fix the problem before it swells.

Match those seams.

# PRESSING MATTERS

There are no hard-and-fast rules about pressing, but a neat, pressed seam is always easier to work with when sewing together blocks.

- Press seams toward the darkest fabric. This should prevent the darker fabric from showing through on the front of the quilt top.

- Press seams to one side when you can, because they are strongest this way. Press seams *open* when you need to reduce bulk, such as when several seams come together.

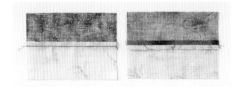

Pressed to the darker side and pressed open

- When faced with adversity, press a seam toward the path of least resistance. If a seam joins multiple seams on one side and only a few on the other, press the seam toward the side with fewer seams to make your life easier.

- Be careful to gently press to reduce the chance of stretching the sewn piece out of shape.

# ADDING BORDERS

The width and number of borders can both add interest and enhance the quilt. It will also increase your quilt's overall size. *The Quilter's Primer* has one dark, skinny inner border and one medium, wider outer border.

The easiest border to learn is called a straight border.

**1.** Measure the longest dimension through the quilt top middle. Do not measure the outer edges, as they may have stretched a bit, which can cause the quilt to become out of "square." Measure the opposite dimension, also through the middle. Add these 2 numbers together and multiply by 2. Decide how wide you want the border to be, including the seam allowances. Multiply this number by 4 and add it to the first total.

For example, a quilt top (before borders are added) measures 40″ × 50″ and the width of the cut borders is 5″.

$$40″ + 50″ = 90″$$

$$90″ × 2 = 180″$$

$$5″ × 4 = 20″$$

$$180″ + 20″ = 200″ \text{ needed for border fabric strips}$$

**2.** Cut strips of border fabric to the desired width. Generally this is best done by cutting across the grain, or from selvage to selvage. Continuing the example above, you need 200″ of border fabric. Your chosen fabric is 42″ wide: 200″ ÷ 42″ = 4.76, therefore you will need to cut 5 strips across the width of the fabric.

**3.** Sew these strips on the short ends with a ¼″ seam allowance. Press the seams open to reduce bulk.

**4.** Cut the 2 longest strips first and sew them to the longest sides of your quilt top. Press the seams outward. *Remeasure* the shorter width (again through the middle), as it is now wider than first measured. Cut 2 strips to this length and sew these to the quilt top. Press the seams outward.

This process can be repeated for additional borders.

# ASSEMBLING A QUILT

## The Quilt Sandwich

A quilt is usually made up of three layers: a pieced top, a middle batting, and a backing.

### BATTING

When purchasing batting, you will have to choose from many types, including polyester, wool, and cotton. Poly/cotton blends are common, but my favorite type is Quilter's Dream 100 percent cotton, because it's reliable, easy to sew, and readily available. Wool batting is wonderfully lightweight and warm. Polyester batting tends to have the highest loft—it's the puffiest. If you are making a quilt intended for a baby, use fire-retardant batting, which is available online and in some quilt shops.

The quilt sandwich

### BACKING

Fabric for the backing is included in the materials list for each project. For larger quilts, you will be instructed to piece the backing. Measurements are listed with the project.

# QUILTING

Quilting refers to sewing together the layers in your sandwich. It can be done by hand, using your home sewing machine, or by a professional quilter.

Personally, if a quilt is larger than a twin size, I send it out to be professionally quilted. If it is twin size or smaller, I do it myself. Hand quilting is an art form in and of itself.

## Quilting by Hand

If you'd like to learn how to hand quilt, check out the books and videos listed under Resources (page 79).

## Machine Quilting at Home

Machine quilting is an art form independent of piecing quilt tops. With practice, machine quilting can be a wonderful addition to your sewing skills.

I've included a tutorial covering the basic steps for straight-line and gentle curves quilting with a walking foot, and simple free-motion quilting. I recommend you check into other sources of information, including the videos and books listed under Resources (page 79).

## SPECIAL TOOLS

Any home sewing machine can be used for quilting any size of quilt, even king. But I recommend starting small—practice on "scrap sandwiches" first.

You'll need a walking foot for your machine, a temporary marking pen, and either a large supply of safety pins or fabric basting spray. You will want a sharp sewing machine needle (perhaps one labeled specially for quilting) and a free-motion foot if you are going to go beyond straight-line quilting. Many people use special quilting gloves, which help you grip the quilt.

**1.** Make a sample quilt sandwich with 2 fabric squares 36″ × 36″ and 1 batting square 36″ × 36″.

**2.** Secure the backing to a hard surface, such as a table or the floor, using masking tape or painter's tape. If working over carpeting, using T-pins might be helpful. Smooth the batting over the backing and then smooth the top over both.

**3.** Baste together the layers using basting spray or safety pins placed every 6″–8″ in all directions. Be sure to pin through all 3 layers. If you're using a temporary basting spray, be sure your working area is well ventilated. Spray the batting, smooth on the backing, turn over the 2 pieces, spray the batting again, and smooth on the top. No pins are necessary if you use basting spray.

**4.** Practice narrowly spaced quilting lines as well as wide, undulating curves in one or two quadrants. Straight lines and gentle curves are easy to master with a walking foot attachment.

Machine quilting with walking foot sample

**5.** To practice free-motion quilting, divide the quilt sandwich into quadrants. Draw a quilting design in one quadrant with a temporary fabric marking pen.

**6.** Start in the middle of an edge and stitch across the drawn quadrant lines. Then, work each quadrant separately to ensure an evenly quilted surface.

**7.** Drop the feed dogs and practice free-motion quilting in another quadrant. Try to keep the stitch length the same while you move the quilt under the needle. This takes lots of practice but can be very rewarding when mastered.

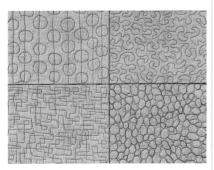
Machine quilting with free-motion foot sample

*tip*

If you can't drop the feed dogs on your machine, cover them with a business card held in place with painter's tape.

## Longarm Quilting

Choosing to send a finished quilt to a professional longarm quilter can be very liberating and satisfying when your quilt is returned to you beautifully quilted. Longarm quilting machines are designed for this one task and do a perfect job, even on a big project. Ask your local fabric shop if they can recommend quilters you can hire.

The following are several factors to consider when deciding whether to quilt yourself or hire a pro:

**1.** How big is the quilt? The larger the quilt, the harder it is to muscle around a home machine.

**2.** How much will it cost? Longarm quilters usually charge by the square inch according to the density of the quilting design you choose. The cost may vary if it is an "edge-to-edge" computer design or if it is a custom, hand-guided design. Don't forget to include the cost of shipping as well as batting or extra thread costs in your calculations.

**3.** How much time will it take? Many longarm quilters are booked months in advance.

Your longarm quilter will have specifications to follow. Generally, longarm quilters require the backing to be 4″–5″ larger than the top. They often have batting available and will want to know what kind and color thread you will want them to use. They often can also bind your quilt for an additional per-inch fee.

# BINDING

After your quilt top is quilted, all that remains is to bind the raw edges and label the back.

## Trim the Quilt Top

**1.** Use the largest square ruler you have to square-up the corners first. This will help with trimming the sides.

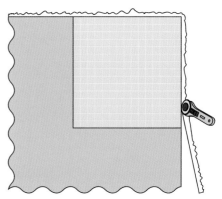
Square-up the quilt corners.

**2.** Use a long ruler to trim each of the 4 sides while joining the squared corners. Then, fold the quilt in half and check that the opposite sides are equal lengths. Repeat to check the other 2 sides, trimming evenly if necessary.

## Add Binding

The edges of a quilt will get the dirtiest and will endure the most stress over time. Binding finishes all the raw edges and frames the quilt top.

*tip*

Double-fold binding is most frequently used to finish quilt edges. Strips cut at 2¼″ will result in a binding that is a bit more than ¼″ wide.

**1.** Piece the binding strips on the bias (diagonal). The pieced strip should be at least 20″ longer than the quilt perimeter.

Sew together binding strips on the diagonal.

**2.** Press the bias seams open.

**3.** Fold the binding in half lengthwise with wrong sides together. Press it very well.

**4.** Place the binding along the right side of the bottom center of the quilt so that the raw edges are aligned. Leaving about a 10″ tail, and using a walking foot, sew the binding to the quilt.

**5.** When you reach a corner, stop ¼″ from the edge, leave the needle down, and pivot the quilt so the corner point is facing you. Reduce the stitch length to very short and sew off the edge on the diagonal.

Stop ¼″ from edge.

Pivot and sew off the corner edge.

**6.** Remove the quilt, turn it 90°, and fold the binding straight up along the diagonal and then down, forming a small fold.

Fold up the binding at the corner.

Fold the binding straight down, aligning the fold with the quilt's edge.

**7.** Continue to sew on the binding. Stop at each corner and repeat Steps 5 and 6.

*tip*

Hold the binding quite taut as you sew, but without stretching it. This will ensure straight, pucker-free edges.

Start at the edge and continue sewing.

**8.** Stop when you have approximately 10″ left to bind. You will have binding tails hanging on each side.

Binding tails

**9.** Fold the 2 binding tails so that they just barely meet with about 1⁄16″ space.

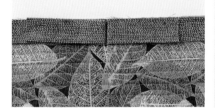

Fold both ends of the binding.

**10.** Crease the fabric along these fold lines. The fold lines on both binding sides will form a cross.

**11.** Line up the 2 crosses and draw a diagonal line as shown. Stitch on this line.

Drawn diagonal stitching line

**12.** Remove all the pins and unfold the binding. Check that the binding fits perfectly; then trim the seam. Finger-press the seam open and attach the final 10″ of binding to the quilt.

Finished splice

**13.** Turn the binding to the wrong side and press it away from the quilt. Sew the binding by hand or machine to the wrong side of the quilt, mitering the corners as shown.

# LABELING A QUILT

Labeling your quilt will give it a personality and value that a store-bought quilt doesn't have. The label can be short and sweet with just your name and the date, or it can be a lengthy story about the recipients, the journey, the place, and so on. I always include my name, place, and year completed.

Embroider your labels by hand or print them on inkjet-ready fabric sheets. There are many ways to make a label, including writing with a permanent fabric ink pen. However you make your labels, they will authenticate your quilts and be appreciated by recipients.

Quilt labels

*tip*

KEEP A QUILTING JOURNAL

Start a quilting journal. Take photos of your finished quilts and write down some details about the process. The choice is yours—fabric selection, the occasion, to whom it was given. If you fall in love with quilting as I have, you will cherish this visual reminder of your quilting journey.

The finished size of each block in *The Quilter's Primer* is 10″ × 10″.

Start building your quiltmaking journey with a simple Rail Fence block. Historically, the Rail Fence was one of the first blocks that young girls learned to make. It was simple to sew and required only scraps.

Select five fabrics that play well together and have a bit of contrast. Choose an order for the colors that you like best and sew the rails together in that order.

## RAIL FENCE BLOCK

Rail Fence block

## Materials

**Fabric A:** 7″ × 7″

**Fabric B:** 7″ × 7″

**Fabric C:** 7″ × 7″

**Fabric D:** 7″ × 7

**Fabric E:** 7″ × 7″

## Cutting

For 1 block:

| FROM | CUT | SIZE |
|---|---|---|
| Fabric A | 4 | 1½″ × 5½″ |
| Fabric B | 4 | 1½″ × 5½″ |
| Fabric C | 4 | 1½″ × 5½″ |
| Fabric D | 4 | 1½″ × 5½″ |
| Fabric E | 4 | 1½″ × 5½″ |

## Make the Block

**1.** Arrange the pieces as shown in the block assembly diagram.

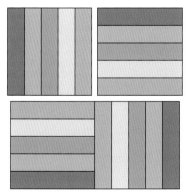

Rail Fence block assembly

**2.** Check your sewing accuracy by piecing a quarter section of the block, pressing all the seams in one direction, and then measuring this section. It should be exactly 5½″ × 5½″ square. If it isn't, make adjustments, referring to Precise Seam Allowances (page 14).

**3.** Finish piecing the remaining 3 quarter sections of the block as directed in Step 2.

**4.** Sew 2 sections together and press the seam toward the long side rail. Repeat with the other 2 sections. Sew together the 2 pairs, matching the center points. Press this seam open and measure the block. It should be exactly 10½″ × 10½″ square. Pat yourself on the back. You've built your first block in the *Primer*.

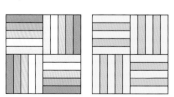

Changing the number of colors or the level of contrast between fabrics can really change the look of a Rail Fence block.

# LOG CABIN BLOCK

Log Cabin block

The Log Cabin block is steeped in history. The design has strong American roots and often features a red center signifying a chimney or the heart of the home. Variations of the Log Cabin block can be seen all over the world in antique textiles. This block is incredibly versatile and should be in every quilter's wheelhouse.

## *tip*

There are dozens of setting possibilities for the Log Cabin block, making it an endless source of entertainment and creativity. Search the Internet for "Log Cabin quilts" to find alternate settings and inspiration.

## Materials

Choose 9 fabrics: 4 lights, 4 darks, and 1 center fabric. (Minimum sizes listed below.)

A center: 3″ × 3″

B dark: 4″ × 4″

C light: 4″ × 5″

D dark: 4″ × 6″

E light: 4″ × 7″

F dark: 4″ × 8″

G light: 4″ × 9″

H dark: 4″ × 10″

I light: 4″ × 11″

## Cutting

For 1 block:

| FROM | CUT | SIZE |
|------|-----|------|
| A center | 1 | 2½″ × 2½″ |
| B dark | 1 | 1½″ × 2½″ |
| B dark and C light | 1 each | 1½″ × 3½″ |
| C light and D dark | 1 each | 1½″ × 4½″ |
| D dark and E light | 1 each | 1½″ × 5½″ |
| E light and F dark | 1 each | 1½″ × 6½″ |
| F dark and G light | 1 each | 1½″ × 7½″ |
| G light and H dark | 1 each | 1½″ × 8½″ |
| H dark and I light | 1 each | 1½″ × 9½″ |
| I light | 1 | 1½″ × 10½″ |

## Make the Block

**1.** Arrange the pieces as shown in the block assembly diagram.

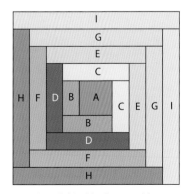

Log Cabin block assembly

**2.** Sew the shortest log to the center square with a scant ¼″ seam. Press the seam away from the center.

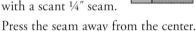

**3.** Continue adding logs in a counter-clockwise direction, minding your scant ¼″ seam. This block will challenge your cutting and sewing accuracy. After each round, press all the seams away from the center.

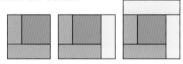

**4.** When completed, your block should measure 10½″ × 10½″ square. If it doesn't, the problem is either the seam allowance or cutting accuracy. If your block is significantly different in size, practice the Precise Seam Allowances (page 14). Small discrepancies really add up—a mere ⅟₁₆″ error on each seam will result in about a 1″ error over the whole block.

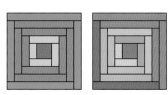

Log Cabin block alternate colorways

# PROJECT:

# RIDE THE RAILS QUILT

**FINISHED QUILT: 62″ × 74″**

Pieced by Dana Hyams,
quilted by Amanda Leins

*Make this quilt with the skills you learned sewing Rail Fence and Log Cabin blocks. The look is different, but the piecing procedures are basically the same. Choose any of the five sizes shown and consider an alternate colorway. Please read through all project directions before cutting your fabric.*

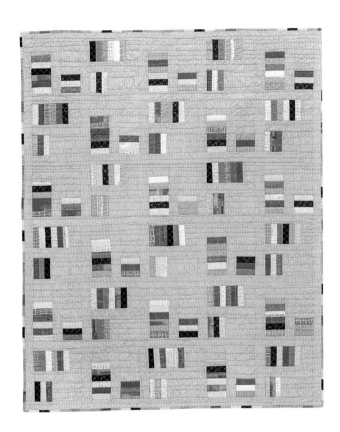

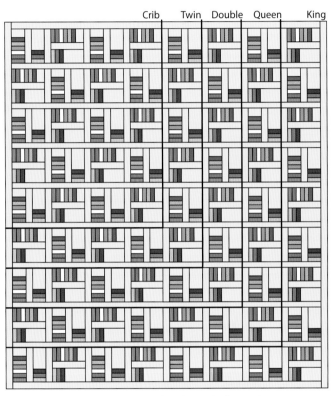

*Ride the Rails* quilt assembly (for multiple sizes)

## Materials

|  | CRIB, 50″ × 62″ | TWIN, 62″ × 74″ | DOUBLE, 74″ × 86″ | QUEEN, 86″ × 98″ | KING, 98″ × 110″ |
|---|---|---|---|---|---|
| Number of blocks | 20 | 30 | 42 | 56 | 72 |
| Background, sashing, and border | 2½ yards | 3⅜ yards | 4¼ yards | 5½ yards | 7 yards |
| Fabric for rails | 9 different fat quarters | 9 different fat quarters | 9 different ⅜-yard cuts | 9 different ½-yard cuts | 9 different ⅝-yard cuts |
| Binding | ½ yard | ⅝ yard | ⅝ yard | ¾ yard | ⅞ yard |
| Batting | Twin/single | Twin/single | Double | Queen | King |
| Backing | 3 yards | 3¾ yards | 5 yards | 7½ yards | 8½ yards |

## Cutting

Cut the number of pieces specified for your desired quilt size.

*WOF = width of fabric*

| | CUT | | | | | SIZE |
|---|---|---|---|---|---|---|
| | Crib | Twin | Double | Queen | King | |
| Background A | 20 | 30 | 42 | 56 | 72 | 3″ × 4½″ |
| Background B | 20 | 30 | 42 | 56 | 72 | 2½″ × 10½″ |
| Background C | 20 | 30 | 42 | 56 | 72 | 4½″ × 6¾″ |
| Background vertical sashing | 15 | 24 | 35 | 48 | 63 | 2½″ × 10½″ |
| Background horizontal sashing and borders | 11 | 15 | 19 | 24 | 30 | 2½″ × WOF |
| Rails: from each of 9 different rail fabrics | 20 each, for a total of 180 rails | 30 each, for a total of 270 rails | 42 each, for a total of 378 rails | 56 each, for a total of 504 rails | 72 each, for a total of 648 rails | 1¾″ × 4½″ |
| Horizontal strip lengths | 6 at 46½″ | 7 at 58½″ | 8 at 70½″ | 9 at 82½″ | 10 at 94½″ | — |
| Side border lengths | 2 at 62½″ | 2 at 74½″ | 2 at 86½″ | 2 at 98½″ | 2 at 110½″ | — |
| Binding | 6 | 7 | 8 | 10 | 11 | 2¼″ × WOF |

# Make the Blocks

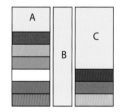

*Ride the Rails* block assembly

**1.** Arrange the pieces needed to build a block as shown in the block assembly diagram.

**2.** Sew the 6 rails together and add background piece A. Press all seams in one direction.

**3.** Sew the 3 rails together and add background piece C. Press all seams in one direction.

**4.** Sew background piece B between the 2 sections made in Steps 2 and 3. Press the seams toward B.

**5.** Press the block and measure. Your block should measure 10½″ × 10½″ square.

**6.** Repeat Steps 1–5 to make the number of blocks for your quilt.

# Make the Quilt Top

*Ride the Rails* row assembly

**1.** Arrange the blocks and vertical sashing strips as shown in the row assembly diagram. Sew together the blocks with vertical sashing to form rows and press the seams toward the sashing.

**2.** Piece the horizontal sashing and borders as needed and cut to the lengths indicated.

**3.** Sew together the pieced rows and the horizontal sashing strips, including the top and bottom borders. Press the seams toward the sashing or borders.

**4.** Attach the side borders and press the seams toward the outside.

**5.** Sew ¼″ around the entire quilt top perimeter to give it stability.

# Finish the Quilt

*For detailed instructions on backing, making a quilt sandwich, quilting, and binding, refer to Quiltmaking Basics (page 13).*

## Backing

Piece the backing for the quilt and trim as needed.

## Sandwich, Quilt, and Bind

**1.** Make a quilt sandwich with the backing, batting, and top.

**2.** Quilt, using the method of your choice.

**3.** Bind and label the quilt.

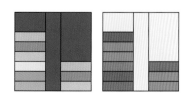

*Ride the Rails* alternate colorways

Sewing on the diagonal can be tricky because fabric is stretchy along the bias. Grab a piece of fabric and try to stretch it selvage to selvage. It doesn't stretch much at all. Now try to stretch it on the diagonal. It has more stretch. That quality can make it hard to sew. This chapter will teach you how to get beautiful results when sewing Flying Geese and half-square triangles.

The Flying Geese block is well known to every quilter. It is one of the most common blocks in both traditional and modern quilts. Search the Internet for "Flying Geese quilts" and be amazed at the variety and versatility of this simple block. There are many ways to build one, but the method taught here is foolproof.

## Materials

Choose your fabrics: 3–5 lights, 1 medium, and 3–5 darks. Or you could use just 1 of each (light, medium, and dark) and sew 10 identical Flying Geese.

Lights: ¼ yard total

Medium: ⅛ yard total

Darks: ¼ yard total

## Cutting

For 1 block:

| FROM | CUT | SIZE |
|---|---|---|
| Lights | 10 | 2½″ × 4½″ |
| Medium | 2 | 1¼″ × 10½″ |
| | 1 | 1″ × 10½″ |
| Darks | 20 | 2½″ × 2½″ |

## FLYING GEESE BLOCK

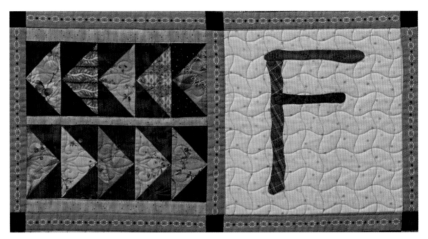

Flying Geese block

## KEY TECHNIQUE: Flying Geese

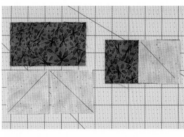

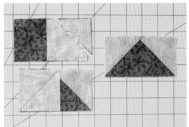

Flying Geese assembly

**1.** Arrange the pieces as shown in the Flying Geese assembly diagrams.

**2.** On the wrong side of the dark squares, draw a diagonal line with a No. 2 pencil or a light-colored pencil if your fabric is very dark. This is your stitching line.

**3.** With right sides together, line up a square with one end of the light 2½″ × 4½″ rectangle, so that the drawn diagonal line is oriented in the correct direction. Stitch on the line. Trim the seam to ¼″ from the stitching, press the seam open, and trim off the excess corners.

**4.** Repeat Step 3 on the opposite end of the light rectangles. Again, pay attention to the orientation of the stitching line. You will be stitching over the previous seam allowance. Trim and press the center triangle seams flat.

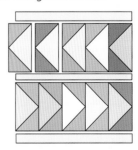

Flying Geese block assembly

## Make the Block

**1.** Sew 10 Flying Geese, using the light rectangles and dark squares

**2.** Sew together 2 sets of 5 Flying Geese as shown in the Flying Geese assembly diagram. Press the seams toward the triangle's base.

**3.** Add the 1″ × 10½″ strip between the 2 sets, and then add the top and bottom strips to make a block. Press the seams toward the strips.

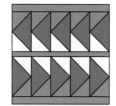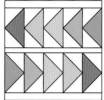

Flying Geese block alternate colorways

# EVENING STAR BLOCK

Evening Star block

The Evening Star block is very versatile, with many options for the center squares. In *The Quilter's Primer*, we will piece a square within a square. You can make this block more easily by cutting a single piece of fabric 5½″ × 5½″ to use for the center. The directions that follow are for the more challenging construction technique.

## Materials

Choose 6 fabrics: 1 light, 1 medium, and 1 dark for the star; another light for the background; 1 medium-dark for the frame; and 1 contrasting for the cornerstones. (Minimum sizes listed below.)

Light star center: 4″ × 7″

Medium star center: 4″ × 4″

Dark star points: 6″ × 11″

Light background: 6″ × 16″

Medium-dark frame: 8″ × 10″

Contrast cornerstones: 4″ × 4″

## Cutting

For 1 block:

| FOR | CUT | SIZE | SUBCUT |
|---|---|---|---|
| Light fabric around center of star | 2 | 2⅞″ × 2⅞″ | Subcut each square once on the diagonal to yield a total of 4 triangles. |
| Medium fabric for star center | 1 | 3⅜″ × 3⅜″ | — |
| Dark fabric for star points | 8 | 2½″ × 2½″ | — |
| Light background fabric | 4<br>4 | 2½″ × 2½″<br>2½″ × 4½″ | — |
| Medium-dark fabric for frame | 4 | 1½″ × 8½″ | — |
| Contrasting fabric for cornerstones | 4 | 1½″ × 1½″ | — |

## Make the Block

*For detailed instructions, refer to Key Technique: Flying Geese (page 25).*

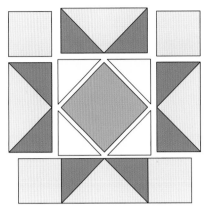

Evening Star center assembly

**1.** Fold each light triangle in half and pinch to make a center crease on the long edge. Fold the large center square in quarters and pinch each edge to mark the center.

**2.** Sew a light triangle to each side of the center square, matching the center creases. Press the seams toward the triangles and trim away the dog-ears.

**3.** Make 4 Flying Geese using the dark 2½″ × 2½″ squares and the background 2½″ × 4½″ rectangles. Stitch on the diagonal lines, trim the seam, flip, press, and trim off the dog-ears.

**4.** Arrange the block as shown in the center assembly diagram. Sew each of the 3 rows and press the first and third row seams outward; press the seams in the second row toward the center.

**5.** Sew the 3 rows together, matching all seams. Press both seams away from the center.

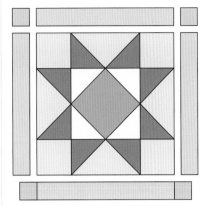

Evening Star frame assembly

**6.** Sew 2 frame strips to either side of the block. Press seams toward the frame.

**7.** Sew the cornerstones to each end of the 2 remaining frame strips. Press the seams toward the frames.

**8.** Sew the frame pieces from Step 7 to the top and bottom of the block. Press the seams toward the frame.

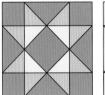 

Evening Star block alternate colorways

# WILD GOOSE CHASE BLOCK

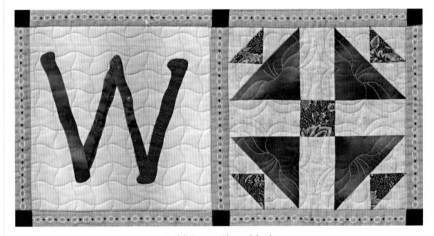

Wild Goose Chase block

The Wild Goose Chase block has several names and is often called Crown of Thorns. It has great possibilities using traditional as well as modern fabrics. The corner triangle element can be a challenge.

## Materials

Choose 3 fabrics: 1 light for the background and 2 medium-darks. (Minimum sizes listed below.)

Light: 12″ × 12″

A medium-dark: 4″ × 10″

B medium-dark: 6″ × 11″

## Cutting

For 1 block:

| FROM | CUT | SIZE | SUBCUT |
|---|---|---|---|
| Light | 4 | 2½″ × 4½″ | — |
| | 6 | 2⅞″ × 2⅞″ | Subcut each square once on the diagonal to yield a total of 12 triangles A. |
| A medium-dark | 2 | 2⅞″ × 2⅞″ | Subcut each square once on the diagonal to yield a total of 4 triangles A. |
| | 1 | 2½″ × 2½″ | — |
| B medium-dark | 2 | 4⅞″ × 4⅞″ | Subcut each square once on the diagonal to yield a total of 4 triangles B. |

## KEY TECHNIQUE: Half-Square Triangles

A great many quilts are based on this simple square that is divided along the diagonal. There are many ways to make half-square triangles, but here's a foolproof method for making these versatile units. Practice making a couple with scrap fabric. Don't toss away those triangle trimmings—sew them into smaller half-square triangle units.

**1.** Cut 2 squares from the 2 fabrics you want to use for your half-square triangle. The size to cut is the exact size you want your finished square to be plus ½″ for the seam allowances. For example, if you want a finished 2″ square, cut the 2 squares 2½″ × 2½″.

**2.** On the wrong side of the lighter square, draw a straight line from corner to corner.

**3.** Stitch on the line and trim the seam ¼″ away.

**4.** Press the seam toward the darker fabric and trim off the dog-ears.

## Make the Block

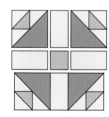

Wild Goose Chase block assembly

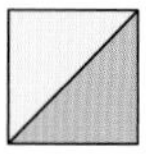

**1.** Match a set of light and medium-dark A triangles and sew together 4 half-square triangle sections as shown.

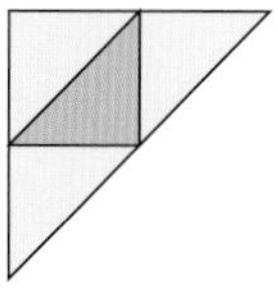

**2.** Add the 2 light A triangles to each half-square triangle from Step 1. Maintain a scant ¼″ seam allowance; otherwise, the end piece will be too small.

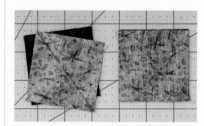

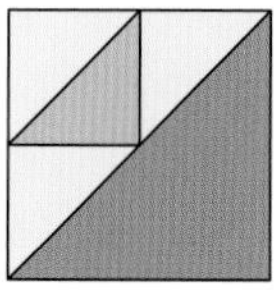

**3.** Sew the large dark B triangle to each unit from Step 2 to make 4 larger pieced squares. Press the seams toward the dark fabric.

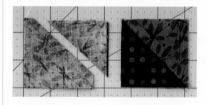

**4.** Sew together each row, pressing the seams toward the dark fabrics.

**5.** Sew together all rows, pressing the seams toward the dark corner triangles.

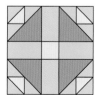

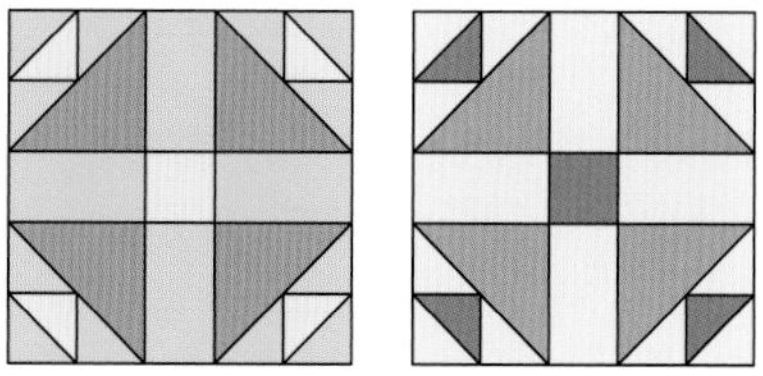

Wild Goose Chase block
alternate colorways

# FLYING GEESE PLACE MAT SET

**FINISHED PLACE MAT: 13″ × 17″**

Pieced by Jane Olsen,
quilted by Janet McWorkman

*These fresh and modern place mats are just the ticket for showcasing some Flying Geese and practicing your newfound sewing skills. Make a set of four and experiment using different color combinations, fabric textures, and prints.*

## Materials

Background: 1 yard

Flying Geese backgrounds: ¼ yard

Flying Geese centers: ¼ yard total if they are all the same; alternately, use a variety of scraps at least 3″ × 5″

Backing: 1 yard

Batting: Crib size is plenty.

Binding: ⅝ yard

## Cutting

Makes 4 place mats.

*WOF = width of fabric*

| FOR | CUT | SIZE |
|---|---|---|
| Background | 4 | 11½″ × 13″ |
| | 8 | 2″ × 4½″ |
| | 4 | 2½″ × 13″ |
| Flying Geese background | 40 | 2½″ × 2½″ |
| Flying Geese center | 20 | 2½″ × 4½″ |
| Backing | 4 | 14″ × 18″ |
| Batting | 4 | 14″ × 18″ |
| Binding | 8 | 2¼″ × WOF |

# Make the Blocks

*For detailed instructions, refer to Key Technique: Flying Geese (page 25).*

**1.** Sew 20 Flying Geese blocks from the 20 center rectangles 2½″ × 4½″ and the 40 Flying Geese background squares 2½″ × 2½″.

**2.** Sew together 4 sets of 5 Flying Geese for each place mat.

**3.** Sew 2 background 2″ × 4½″ rectangles to the top and bottom of the Flying Geese units.

**4.** Sew the narrow rectangle to the left side of the Flying Geese and the wider rectangle to the right side.

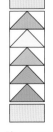

Place mat assembly

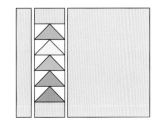

**5.** Square-up each place mat top to 13″ × 17″.

# Finish the Place Mats

*For detailed instructions on making a quilt sandwich, quilting, and binding, refer to Quiltmaking Basics (page 13).*

## Sandwich, Quilt, and Bind

**1.** Make quilt sandwiches from the backing, batting, and tops.

**2.** Quilt, using the method of your choice. The place mat set shown was quilted on a home machine using Aurifil 40-weight thread in straight lines spaced ½″ apart.

**3.** Sew together 2 binding strips for each place mat. Bind the place mats.

Challenge yourself with the next three blocks by working with both smaller pieces and diagonals. Accuracy is key—it becomes increasingly important to be spot on when cutting and sewing these blocks. You will be using both strip piecing and templates.

## *tip*

The Northern Star block in *The Quilter's Primer* features several darks and lights; however, the effect will not be lost by using only one of each.

# NORTHERN STAR BLOCK

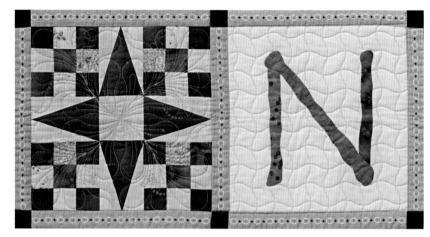

Northern Star block

## Materials

Choose 2 fabrics. (Minimum sizes listed below.)

A light: 10˝ × 15˝

B dark: 14˝ × 16˝

## Cutting

*Use Northern Star patterns A and B (pullout page P2) to make templates A, B, and B-reversed. (B-reversed is piece B flipped over in the reverse direction.) For detailed instructions, refer to Key Technique: Make a Template (page 31).*

For 1 block:

| FROM | CUT | SIZE |
|---|---|---|
| A light | 1 | 1¾˝ × 15˝ |
| | 2 | 1¾˝ × 8˝ |
| | 4 | Template B |
| | 4 | Template B-reversed |
| B dark | 1 | 3˝ × 3˝ |
| | 2 | 1¾˝ × 15˝ |
| | 1 | 1¾˝ × 8˝ |
| | 4 | Template A |

# Make the Block

*For detailed instructions, refer to Key Technique: Make a Nine-Patch (page 31).*

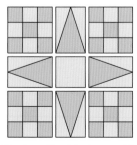

Northern Star block assembly

### NINE-PATCH UNITS

**1.** Sew 2 dark 1¾˝ × 15˝ strips to either side of a light 1¾˝ × 15˝ strip. Press the seams toward the dark fabric. Subcut the strip set into 8 units each 1¾˝ wide.

**2.** Sew 2 light 1¾˝ × 8˝ strips to either side of a dark 1¾˝ × 8˝ strip.

Press the seams toward the dark fabric. Subcut this strip set into 4 units each 1¾˝ wide.

**3.** Sew 2 units from Step 1 to either side of a unit from Step 2 to make a nine-patch unit.

**4.** Repeat Steps 1–3 to make a total of 4 units.

## STAR POINTS

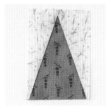

Finished Northern Star point

**1.** Arrange 4 star points A, 4 star backgrounds B, and 4 star backgrounds B-reversed.

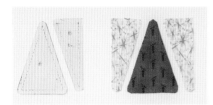

Arrange star points and backgrounds.

**2.** Sew a star background to either side of a star point. Press the seams open. Make 4.

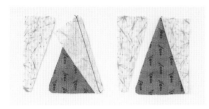

## FINISH THE BLOCK

**1.** Arrange units and center square as shown in the Northern Star block assembly diagram (page 30).

**2.** Sew each row together, pressing the seams toward the star points.

**3.** Sew the rows together and press the seams toward the star points.

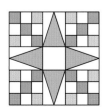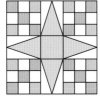

Northern Star block alternate colorways

## KEY TECHNIQUE: Make a Template

Templates can be made of paper, cardboard, or a sturdier plastic sheet. When a template will be used many times, I prefer to make it out of template plastic.

**1.** Place the template plastic sheet over the paper pattern and trace the shape using a thin Sharpie pen or other dark marker that doesn't smudge. Use a ruler for any straight lines.

**2.** Cut out the template exactly on the traced line.

## KEY TECHNIQUE: Make a Nine-Patch

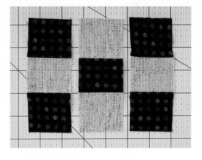

Nine-Patch unit

**1.** Sew together 2 sets of 3 strips, alternating dark-light-dark and light-dark-light.

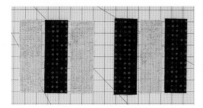

**2.** Press the seams toward the darker fabric.

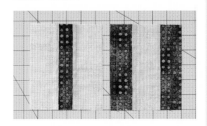

**3.** Trim an edge of both strip sets to neaten the edges, if needed.

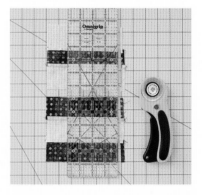

**4.** Cut strips and arrange the alternating cut strips as shown.

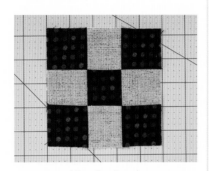

The pressed seams will nest on the reverse side.

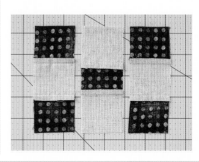

# VIRGINIA REEL BLOCK

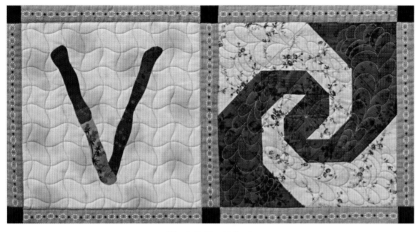

Quilt historians like to debate correct names and color placement for this block. One version is called Snails Trail, and some designs incorporate half-square triangles. We'll learn one version for *The Quilter's Primer* and a modified one for a small quilt project that uses an alternate piecing and color placement that looks like rolling waves.

Virginia Reel block

## Materials

Choose 1 light and 1 dark fabric.

**A light:** 12″ × 14″

**B dark:** 12″ × 14″

## Make the Block

**1.** Arrange the pieces as shown in the block assembly diagram.

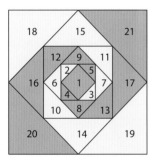

Virginia Reel block assembly

**2.** Starting with the center square and working in numerical order, sew pairs of triangles to opposite sides of the center.

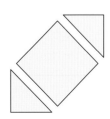

## Cutting

For 1 block:

| FROM | CUT | SIZE | SUBCUT |
|------|-----|------|--------|
| A light | 1 | 5⅞″ × 5⅞″ | Subcut diagonally to yield 2 triangles each. |
| B dark | 1 | | |
| A light | 1 | 6¼″ × 6¼″ | Subcut diagonally twice to yield 4 triangles each. (There will be 2 extra of each.) |
| B dark | 1 | | |
| A light | 1 | 3⅜″ × 3⅜″ | Subcut diagonally to yield 2 triangles each. |
| B dark | 1 | | |
| A light | 1 | 3¾″ × 3¾″ | Subcut diagonally twice to yield 4 triangles each. (There will be 2 extra of each.) |
| B dark | 1 | | |
| A light | 1 | 2⅛″ × 2⅛″ | Subcut diagonally to yield 2 triangles each. |
| B dark | 1 | | |
| B dark center | 1 | 1¾″ × 1¾″ | — |

**3.** Press all seams outward from the center square after each set of 2 triangles.

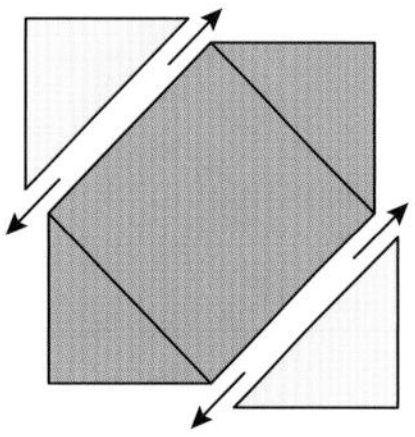

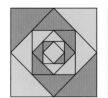

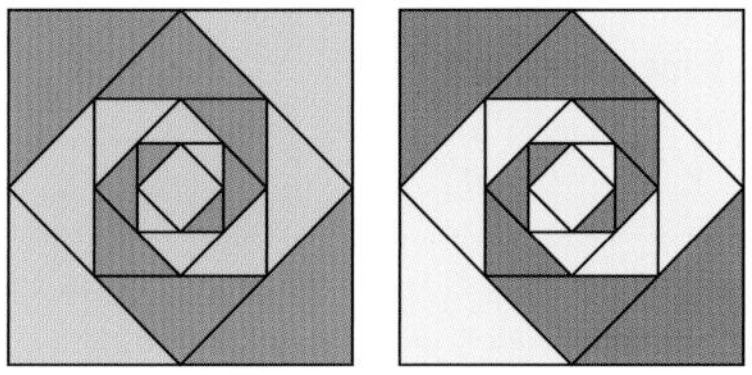

Virginia Reel block alternate colorways

# APPLE CORE BLOCK

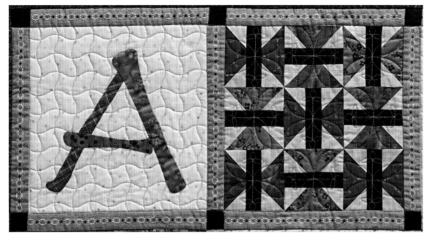

Apple Core block

This block is composed of 63 pieces. Sound daunting? You can do this! Organize all the components prior to sewing. The apple core corners will be sewn using a method that is similar to half-square triangles.

*tip*

COLOR NOTES

*The Quilter's Primer* uses muddy reds for the apple components and dark browns for the core. Feel free to play with color placement. This block will work as long as there is a clear distinction between the light, medium, and dark fabrics.

## Materials

Choose 5 fabrics: 1 dark, 1 light, and 3 mediums. (Minimum sizes listed below.)

Dark apple core: 9″ × 10″

A medium apple: 5″ × 12″

B medium apple: 5″ × 12″

C medium apple: 5″ × 12″

Light background: 11″ × 11″

## Cutting

For 1 block:

| FROM | CUT | SIZE |
|---|---|---|
| Dark apple core | 9 | 1⅝″ × 3⅞″ |
| A medium apple | 6 | 1⅝″ × 3⅞″ |
| B medium apple | 6 | |
| C medium apple | 6 | |
| Light background | 36 | 1⅝″ × 1⅝″ |

## Make the Block

Apple Core block assembly

**1.** Mark a diagonal line on the back of each background square.

**2.** Place a square at each end of an apple rectangle, noting the placement of the diagonal.

**3.** Sew along the diagonal line. Trim the seam and press toward the darker fabric. Make 18.

**4.** Sew pairs of Step 3 units to either side of the apple core rectangles. Press the seams toward the center.

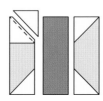

Apple Core component blocks; make 9.

**5.** Arrange the small component blocks as shown in the assembly diagram. Sew together 3 blocks to make each row. Press the seams in rows 1 and 3 away from the center. Press the seams in row 2 toward the center. Sew together the rows, being careful to match the corners. Press the seams to one side.

*tip*

Use a dab of glue stick to get all eight fabrics to play nicely where lots of seams come together. Be sure it is washable glue, such as Elmer's.

Apple Core block
alternate colorways

# REEL TIME THROW

**FINISHED QUILT: 40″ × 50″**

Pieced by Janet McWorkman,
quilted by Terri Wangstrom

Reel Time *is a throw-sized quilt with a design that capitalizes on the block's wave appearance. It uses a light, a dark, and a contrast color for the wave. Use a single fabric for C or a variety like I did.*

## Materials

**Fabric A:** 1⅝ yards for narrow background, blocks, and binding

**Fabric B:** 1⅝ yards for wide background, blocks, and binding

**Fabric C:** ⅝ yard for blocks

**Batting:** Crib size

**Backing:** 2½ yards

## Cutting

*Cut the background and binding rectangles first. LOF = length of fabric*

| BLOCK PIECE | FROM | CUT | SIZE | SUBCUT |
|---|---|---|---|---|
| Left background | A | 1 | 10½″ × 50½″ | — |
| Right background | B | 1 | 20½″ × 50½″ | — |
| Binding | A | 2 | 2¼″ × LOF strips | — |
| | B | 2 | 2¼″ × LOF strips | |
| | C | 2 | 2¼″ × 6″ | |
| 16 | A | 2 | 6¼″ × 6¼″ | Subcut diagonally twice to yield 4 triangles each. |
| 17 | B | 2 | | |
| 14 and 15 | C | 3 | | |
| 20 | A | 3 | 5⅞″ × 5⅞″ | Subcut diagonally to yield 2 triangles each. |
| 21 | B | 3 | | |
| 18 and 19 | C | 5 | | |
| 9 | A | 2 | 3¾″ × 3¾″ | Subcut diagonally twice to yield 4 triangles each. |
| 8 | B | 2 | | |
| 6 and 7 | C | 3 | | |
| 12 | A | 3 | 3⅜″ × 3⅜″ | Subcut diagonally to yield 2 triangles each. |
| 13 | B | 3 | | |
| 10 and 11 | C | 5 | | |
| 22 | A | 5 | 3⅜″ × 3⅜″ | — |
| 23 | B | 5 | | |
| 5 | A | 3 | 2⅛″ × 2⅛″ | Subcut diagonally to yield 2 triangles each. |
| 4 | B | 3 | | |
| 2 and 3 | C | 5 | | |
| 1 | C | 5 | 1¾″ × 1¾″ | — |

# Make the Blocks

*For detailed instructions, refer to Key Technique: Half-Square Triangles (page 28).*

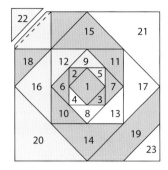

Reel Time block assembly

Sew 5 blocks as shown in the block assembly diagram. Please note that on this version, you'll be adding a half-square triangle to the corner.

# Make the Quilt Top

**1.** Arrange the blocks and large rectangles as shown in the quilt assembly diagram.

**2.** Sew the blocks together and press all the seams in one direction. Be mindful of each block's wavelike orientation.

**3.** Sew the rectangles to each side of the block unit, pressing the seams toward the rectangles.

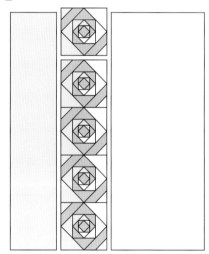

*Reel Time* quilt assembly

# Finish the Quilt

*For detailed instructions, refer to Quiltmaking Basics (page 13).*

**1.** Make a quilt sandwich with the backing, batting, and top.

**2.** Quilt, using the method of your choice.

**3.** Piece the binding to match the backgrounds and block edges. Bind the quilt.

**4.** Label and love.

This chapter is all about working with many small pieces. You will also learn foundation piecing.

The Pickets and Posts block is built using two templates for the picket points. I simplified the block, using rectangles for the posts and only three fabrics.

## Materials

Choose 3 fabrics: 1 light and 2 medium darks. (Minimum sizes listed below.)

**Light background:** 12″ × 13″

**A medium dark:** 11″ × 15″ for tall picket points and posts

**B medium dark:** 7″ × 10″ for short picket points and posts

## Cutting

*Use Picket patterns A and B (pullout page P1) to make templates A, B, and B-reversed. Refer to Key Technique: Make a Template (page 31). Template B-reversed (Br) is piece B flipped over in the reverse direction.*

Makes 1 block.

| FROM | CUT | SIZE |
|------|-----|------|
| Light background | 10 | Template B |
| | 10 | Template B-reversed |
| | 4 | 2½″ × 2½″ |
| A medium dark | 6 | Template A |
| B medium dark | 4 | |
| A medium dark | 3 | 2½″ × 6½″ |
| B medium dark | 2 | 2½″ × 2½″ |

# PICKETS AND POSTS BLOCK

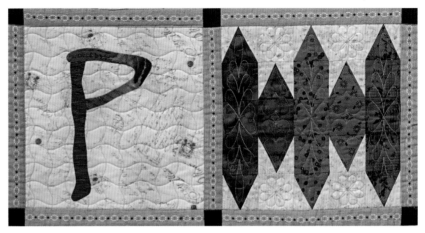

Pickets and Posts block

## Make the Block

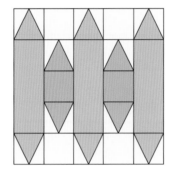

Pickets and Posts block assembly

**1.** Sew 1 light triangle B and 1 light triangle Br to either side of each medium-dark picket point A. Press seams away from A. Repeat this step to make 10 pickets total.

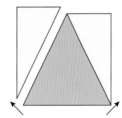

**2.** Sew 2 matching picket points to each tall picket post. Press the seams toward the posts.

**3.** Sew background squares to each point of the remaining picket points; then sew the picket points to the short posts. Press the seams toward the posts.

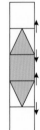

**4.** Arrange the 5 pickets as shown in the block assembly diagram. Sew all 4 seams and press them toward the long posts.

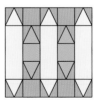 

Pickets and Posts block alternate colorways

# ZIGZAG BLOCK

Here's a block with small pieces, sharp points, and bias edges. We'll use foundation paper piecing to make it go together accurately and easily. Foundation piecing isn't the most economical use of fabric, but the benefit of a perfect block is very satisfying. You'll need an Add-A-Quarter ruler. This block finishes 5″ × 5″ and will be combined with the Yo-Yo block (page 71) and the Y and Z appliqué blocks (page 72) to create a 10″ × 10″ finished block for *The Quilter's Primer* quilt.

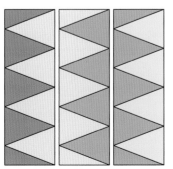

Zigzag block

## Materials

Choose 2 fabrics: 1 light and 1 dark. (Minimum sizes listed below.)

Light: 10″ × 11″

Dark: 10″ × 11″

## Cutting

Makes 1 block.

| FROM | CUT | SIZE |
|---|---|---|
| Light fabric | 13 | 2″ × 3″ |
| Dark fabric | 14 | 2″ × 3″ |

## Make the Block

*Make three copies of the Zigzag foundation pattern (pullout page P1); each copy will be used to make one unit. You will be directed to make two identical units and another with the colors placement reversed. For detailed instructions on paper piecing, refer to Key Technique: Foundation Paper Piecing (page 38).*

Zigzag block assembly

**1.** Using the Zigzag foundation pattern and starting with the dark fabric, sew together a unit, alternating the darks and lights.

**2.** Repeat Step 1, making an identical unit.

**3.** For the third unit, repeat Step 1, but start with the light fabric and continue alternating the fabrics.

**4.** Press all units lightly and trim them to size, using the paper as your guide.

**5.** Carefully remove the paper foundation from the backs of the units.

*tip*

Prevent pulled stitches by pinching the edges where seams start.

**6.** Sew together the units as shown, creating a zigzag effect and making a square 5″ × 5″. Press the block.

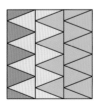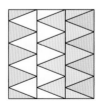

Zigzag block
alternate colorways

*tip* — FOUNDATION PIECING TIPS

- Get online and head over to wikiHow, Craftsy, About.com, or YouTube for video tutorials on foundation piecing. Seeing is believing!

- Study the block assembly diagrams and work first with scrap fabric.

- Shorten the stitch length to 1.5 mm or 18 stitches per inch. You want your stitches to be very close together.

- Use a size 14/90 needle to make large perforations in the paper.

- A junk-mail postcard placed on the seamlines makes a great straightedge for folding foundation paper out of the way.

- Use tweezers as needed to remove the paper foundation after piecing.

- Carol Doak's Foundation Paper (by C&T Publishing) is printable and tears away easily.

**1.** Make 1 or 2 copies of the foundation pattern for practice.

**2.** Align the first fabric with the seamline between sections 1 and 2 on the paper piece, adding a ¼" seam allowance. The wrong side of the fabric should be next to the wrong (unprinted) side of the paper foundation, and the first section (number 1) should be covered completely. Pin the fabric in place.

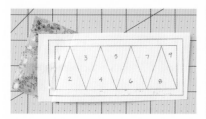

**3.** Add the second fabric, lining it up with the first. It is helpful to place a straightedge on the stitching line when folding the paper foundation away.

**4.** Sew on the stitching line. Be sure to use a very short stitch length.

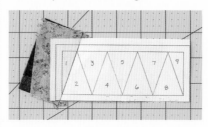

**5.** Place the Add-A-Quarter ruler right up next to the paper fold and trim both seam allowances at one time.

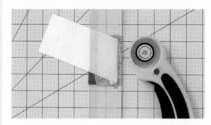

**6.** Press the seam and add the third fabric as in Steps 3 and 4. When adding additional fabric pieces, it might be necessary to make small tears in the paper foundation when you fold the foundation away.

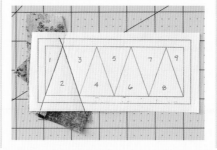

**7.** Trim with the Add-A-Quarter ruler after stitching each seam. Continue adding fabric pieces in numerical order.

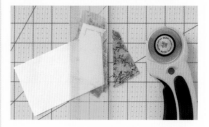

**8.** After sewing together all the pieces, press the unit and trim excess fabric on the seam allowance line.

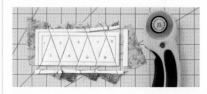

**9.** Remove the paper foundation.

**10.** The right side of a finished Zigzag unit should look like this.

# Xquisite Block

The Xquisite block looks very complicated, since it involves many small pieces. When broken down into steps, however, it is really quite simple to sew together. Organize your fabrics prior to cutting and be mindful of your color placement to get the best visual effect.

Xquisite block

## Materials

Choose 7 fabrics: 1 dark and 1 light for the corner triangles, 2 medium lights, and 3 medium darks.

Dark corners: 8″ × 8″

Light corners: 8″ × 8″

A medium dark: 7″ × 7″

B medium dark: 4″ × 7″

C medium dark: 7″ × 7″

A medium light: 7″ × 7″

B medium light: 7″ × 7″

## Cutting

Makes 1 block.

| FROM | CUT | SIZE |
|---|---|---|
| Dark corners | 16 | 1¾″ × 1¾″ |
| Light corners | 16 | 1¾″ × 1¾″ |
| A medium dark | 4 | 3″ × 3″ |
| B medium dark | 2 | 3″ × 3″ |
| C medium dark | 3 | 3″ × 3″ |
| A medium light | 4 | 3″ × 3″ |
| B medium light | 3 | 3″ × 3″ |

## Make the Block

*For detailed instructions, refer to Key Technique: Half-Square Triangles (page 28).*

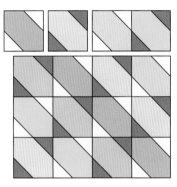

Xquisite block assembly

**1.** Referring to the block assembly diagram, arrange the 3″ × 3″ squares in a 4 × 4 grid.

**2.** Add pairs of the dark and light corner squares to each 3″ × 3″ square.

**3.** Sew the pairs of corner squares to opposite corners of each of the 16 squares.

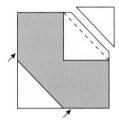

Xquisite unit assembly

**4.** Trim the excess corners ¼″ from the seams and press the seams toward the larger square.

**5.** Place the 16 squares back into the block arrangement. Sew 4 rows of 4 squares. Press the seams in each row in opposite directions.

**6.** Sew the rows together, matching the seams, and give the block a final, gentle pressing.

Xquisite block alternate colorways

# PICKETS AND POSTS TABLE RUNNER

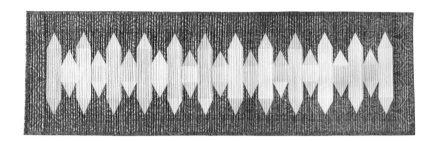

**FINISHED TABLE RUNNER: 14″ × 50″**

Pieced and quilted by Lisa Bauer

*This table runner is very fun to make. Change the length to fit your table, or use the pattern to make place mats. You can choose just one white fabric for all the pickets and posts or "scrap it" by mixing a range of whites, as in the sample project. Use the same templates you made for the Pickets and Posts block (pullout page P1).*

## Materials

Assorted whites: 4 fat quarters or ⅝ yard total

Background and border: 1⅛ yards

Backing: 1½ yards

Batting: Crib size is plenty.

Binding: ⅜ yard

## Cutting

Makes all blocks.

*WOF = width of fabric*

| FOR | CUT | SIZE |
|---|---|---|
| Pickets and posts from the assorted whites | 46 | Template A |
| | 11 | 2½″ × 2½″ |
| | 12 | 2½″ × 6½″ |
| Background | 46 | Template B |
| | 46 | Template B-reversed |
| Borders | 3 | 2½″ × WOF |
| Binding | 4 | 2¼″ × WOF |

# Make the Top

*Use Picket patterns A and B (pullout page P1) to make templates A, B, and Br. Template Br is piece B flipped over in the reverse direction. For detailed instructions, refer to Pickets and Posts Block (page 36).*

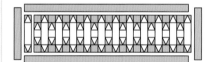

*Pickets and Posts assembly*

**1.** Make 23 posts with picket points, following the directions for Pickets and Posts Block (page 36). (Do not sew the assembled posts into blocks yet.)

**2.** Arrange all 23 units, starting and ending with a tall post and alternating tall and short posts for the entire length of the table runner.

**3.** When you're satisfied with the layout, sew together the posts. Press the seams toward the tall posts.

# Finish

*For detailed instructions on making a quilt sandwich, quilting, and binding, refer to Quiltmaking Basics (page 13).*

## Borders

**1.** Sew the border strips end to end and press the seams open.

**2.** Cut 2 border strips 2½″ × 46½″ and 2 borders strips 2½″ × 14½″.

**3.** Sew a long border strip to each long side. Press the seams toward the borders.

**4.** Sew the remaining 2 borders to the short ends and press the seams toward the borders. Press.

## Backing

Cut the backing 16″ × 52″.

## Sandwich, Quilt, and Bind

**1.** Make a quilt sandwich with the backing, batting, and top.

**2.** Quilt, using the method of your choice. The *Pickets and Posts table runner* was quilted with Aurifil 40-weight white thread at ¼″ intervals.

**3.** Bind and label the table runner.

The next four blocks are more challenging. The Inner City block is a half-hexagon design that relies on thoughtful color and value placement to achieve a three-dimensional effect. The Bargello block also uses color and value to create waves of pattern. The Kansas Troubles and School House blocks involve many different sizes of small pieces. Cut, sew, and arrange colors carefully, and you will be rewarded with beautiful blocks.

The Inner City block uses strip piecing, a template, and a new technique: set-in seams. Don't get scared off; you can do this. You will be instructed to make the block a bit larger than needed to give you a bit of fudge room when trimming down to a 10½″ × 10½″ square. This is a great block for using up scraps.

## Materials

This block achieves its three-dimensional effect with clear value changes. In *The Quilter's Primer*, I used red, blue, green, brown, and yellow hues in light, medium, and dark values for a total of 18 fabrics. You can reduce the number of colors used but not the number of values—include a light, medium, and dark in each color grouping. The cutting chart represents all 6 colors used in *The Quilter's Primer*. You will need at least one pair of rectangles in each fabric.

# INNER CITY BLOCK

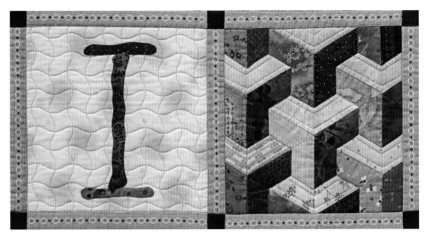

Inner City block

## Cutting

Makes 1 block.

| FROM | CUT | SIZE |
|---|---|---|
| Light red (pink) | 2 | 2″ × 4″ |
| Medium red | 3 | 2″ × 4″ |
| Dark red | 3 | 2″ × 4″ |
| Light blue | 2 | 2″ × 4″ |
| Medium blue | 2 | 2″ × 4″ |
| Dark blue | 2 | 2″ × 4″ |
| Light green | 2 | 2″ × 4″ |
| Medium green | 2 | 2″ × 4″ |
| Dark green | 2 | 2″ × 4″ |
| Light brown | 4 | 2″ × 4″ |
| Medium brown | 4 | 2″ × 4″ |
| Dark brown | 4 | 2″ × 4″ |
| Light yellow | 2 | 2″ × 4″ |
| Medium yellow | 2 | 2″ × 4″ |
| Dark yellow | 2 | 2″ × 4″ |
| Light gray-brown | 2 | 2″ × 4″ |
| Medium gray-brown | 2 | 2″ × 4″ |
| Dark gray-brown | 2 | 2″ × 4″ |

## Make the Block

*Use the Inner City pattern (pullout page P1) to make a template. For instructions on making a template, refer to Key Technique: Making a Template (page 31). For detailed instructions on sewing together the rows, refer to Key Technique: Set-In Seams (page 42).*

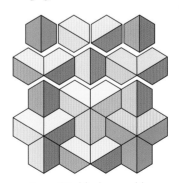

Inner City block assembly

**1.** Take a good look at the diagram and arrange your fabrics into 22 fabric pairings. The pairs will be light-dark, light-medium, and medium-dark. Take your time at this stage to create a three-dimensional effect. Note that all the lights are on the top and all the darks are on the right.

**2.** Sew together all the pairs from Step 1, making 22 rectangles 3½″ × 4″. Press the seams open.

**3.** Line up the centerline on the Inner City hexagon template with the center seam on a rectangle made in Step 2. Cut the hexagon. (The template pattern includes a seam allowance.) Repeat this step to cut 22 hexies.

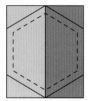

**4.** Arrange the 22 hexie units as shown in the block assembly diagram, keeping the values in the proper orientation.

**5.** Sew together each row of hexie units side by side. Press the seams open to reduce bulk.

**6.** To sew together the rows, you will need to sew set-in seams. See Key Technique: Set-In Seams (at right).

**7.** Trim the block to 10½″ × 10½″ square.

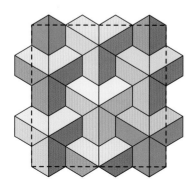

Squaring-up the Inner City block

## KEY TECHNIQUE: Set-In Seams

Use the hexagon pattern from the Inner City block (pullout page P1).

**1.** Choose 3 hexies. Include a light, medium, and dark in the set.

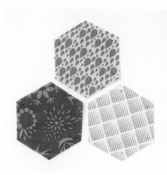

**2.** Place 2 hexies right sides together. On one edge, mark points ¼″ in from both ends. Sew together the hexies, starting and stopping on the marked points.

**3.** Add a third hexie below the pair. Repeat Step 2 and attach the third hexie to one of the other hexies, again sewing only from point to point and folding the attached hexie out of the way while you sew.

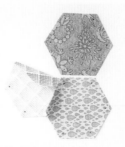

**4.** Using the same technique, sew together the 2 hexies that are not yet attached, being sure to start and stop at the marked points. Press all the seams open.

Wrong side of hexie triad

Right side of hexie triad

**5.** When sewing rows of hexies together, you will use the same technique, sewing each seam individually.

# KANSAS TROUBLES BLOCK

The first known mention of Kansas Troubles as a quilt block was in 1890. The name refers to the struggle in that state while achieving statehood. However, I can't help but think those Kansas ladies had trouble hand piecing this block with so many small half-square triangles! High contrast between the light and dark half-square triangles makes this block interesting.

Kansas Troubles block

## Materials

*Note: The Kansas Troubles block in* The Quilter's Primer *includes a border, but the version here does not.*

Choose 4 fabrics with distinct values: 1 very light, 1 medium light, 1 medium dark, and 1 very dark. (Minimum sizes listed below.)

Very light: 5″ × 13″     Medium dark: 5″ × 10″

Medium light: 7″ × 13″     Very dark fabric: 5″ × 14″

## Cutting

For 1 block:

| FROM | CUT | SIZE | SUBCUT |
|---|---|---|---|
| Very light | 4 | 1¾″ × 1¾″ | — |
| | 8 | 2⅛″ × 2⅛″ | Subcut each diagonally for a total of 16 triangles. |
| Medium light | 2 | 5⅞″ × 5⅞″ | Subcut each diagonally for a total of 4 triangles. |
| Medium dark | 2 | 3⅜″ × 3⅜″ | Subcut each diagonally for a total of 4 triangles. |
| Very dark | 12 | 2⅛″ × 2⅛″ | Subcut each diagonally for a total of 24 triangles. |

## Make the Block

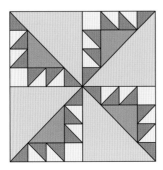

Kansas Troubles block assembly

**1.** Pair up and sew 16 sets of very light and very dark small triangles on the diagonals to make 16 half-square triangle units. Press the seams toward the dark triangle.

**2.** Refer to the Kansas Troubles assembly diagram and sew the half-square triangle units made in Step 1 into 8 pairs. Make 4 units with dark triangles in the upper left and 4 units with dark triangles in the upper right. All 8 pairs are not sewn with the diagonals placed exactly the same way.

**3.** Sew a very dark triangle to 4 of the half-square triangle units. Watch the placement of that dark triangle. It is very easy to get it on the wrong side or turned the wrong way.

**4.** Sew the short side of a medium-dark triangle to 4 of the half-square triangle units. Press the seams toward the medium-dark triangle.

**5.** Sew a very dark triangle on one end of the remaining 4 half-square triangle units and the very light square on the opposite end.

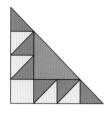

**6.** Sew together a unit from Step 4 and a unit from Step 5. Repeat 3 more times.

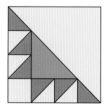

**7.** Sew the medium-light triangles to the units completed in Step 6 to make 4 squares. Press seams toward the largest triangle. These units should measure 5½" × 5½".

**8.** Sew the 4 squares together to complete the block. Give it a gentle pressing and pat yourself on the back! This was a challenging block to build.

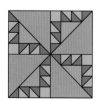

Kansas Troubles block
alternate colorways

# BARGELLO BLOCK

Bargello block

Bargello is a special piecing method that results in beautiful, undulating waves of color. One of the nice things about this technique is that it's actually much easier than it looks, as long as you choose your fabrics well. A smooth gradation of values from lightest to darkest is the key to achieving the block's visual movement.

| Materials and Cutting | |
|---|---|
| Lightest fabric 1 | 1¾" × 20" |
| Fabric 2 | 1¾" × 20" |
| Fabric 3 | 1¾" × 20" |
| Fabric 4 | 1¾" × 20" |
| Fabric 5 | 1¾" × 20" |
| Fabric 6 | 1¾" × 20" |
| Fabric 7 | 1¾" × 20" |
| Darkest fabric 8 | 1¾" × 20" |

*tip*

Place 8–12 fabrics in a light-to-dark gradation and snap a black-and-white photo with a phone or camera. Fabrics that are misplaced will stand out.

## Make the Block

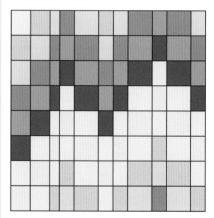

Bargello block assembly

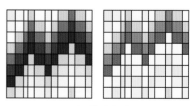

Bargello block
alternate colorways

## KEY TECHNIQUE: Bargello

**1.** Sew together the 8 fabric strips in order from light to dark.

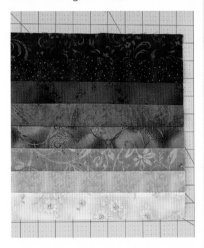

*tip*

Use a very short stitch length (1.2 mm or 20 stitches per inch) when sewing together the strips so that they don't come apart later in the process when you cut the strips into small widths.

**2.** Press the seams in alternating directions.

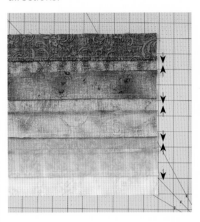

**3.** Square-up a pieced edge of the strip set.

**4.** Sew the strip set into a tube by sewing the lightest and the darkest strips together.

**5.** Subcut the strip set into widths as specified in the chart.

| BARGELLO SUBCUTTING | CUT | WIDTH |
|---|---|---|
| A | 2 | 1½˝ |
| B | 5 | 1¼˝ |
| C | 3 | 1¾˝ |
| D | 1 | 1˝ |

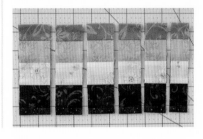

**6.** Using a seam ripper, separate each cut tube into a strip by carefully removing the stitches between the 2 fabrics noted in the chart (at right). Keep the strips in this order.

| Cut strips | A | A | D | B | C | B | B | C | B | C | B |
|---|---|---|---|---|---|---|---|---|---|---|---|
| Remove stitches between | 2–3 | 3–4 | 4–5 | 5–6 | 4–5 | 3–4 | 4–5 | 5–6 | 6–7 | 5–6 | 4–5 |

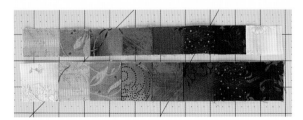

**7.** Sew together the strip sets from left to right. It is helpful to sew a *very* scant ¼˝ seam, as the Bargello method tends to eat up fabric. Press all the seams in one direction and check that the block is square. (If your block is too narrow, the easy fix is to add another strip set to one side and then trim as needed.)

# SCHOOL HOUSE BLOCK

The School House block is one of my personal favorites. If you search the web for these blocks, you will discover an enormous variety of quilted styles, from midcentury modern to simple designs built from only four pieces. The traditional School House block featured in *The Quilter's Primer* is complicated. There are many pieces of different sizes. Organization at this point will make your life much easier when sewing together these small pieces.

School House block

## Materials

Choose 3 fabrics: 1 light and 1 dark. (Minimum sizes listed below.)

Background: 6″ × 15″

House walls: 8″ × 12″

Roof: 6″ × 10″

Windows and door: 4″ × 8″

Chimneys: 3″ × 4″

## Cutting

Makes 1 block.

| FOR | CUT | SIZE |
|---|---|---|
| Background | 4 | 2½″ × 2½″ |
| | 1 | 2½″ × 3½″ |
| | 1 | 2½″ × 4½″ |
| | 1 | 1½″ × 5½″ |
| | 1 | 1½″ × 6½″ |
| House walls | 4 | 1½″ × 5½″ |
| | 1 | 1½″ × 4½″ |
| | 3 | 1½″ × 3½″ |
| | 1 | 1½″ × 2½″ |
| | 2 | 1½″ × 1½″ |
| Roof | 4 | 2½″ × 2½″ |
| | 1 | 2½″ × 3½″ |
| Windows and door | 4 | 1½″ × 1½″ |
| | 1 | 1½″ × 2½″ |
| | 1 | 2½″ × 3½″ |
| Chimney | 2 | 1½″ × 2½″ |

# Make the Block

*For detailed instructions, refer to Key Technique: Half-Square Triangles (page 28).*

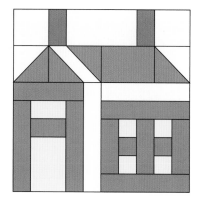

School House block assembly

**1.** Arrange all the pieces for the block as shown in the assembly diagram.

**2.** Begin with the chimney section. Sew the 2 chimney strips to each end of the background 2½″ × 4½″ rectangle. Add 2 background squares 2½″ × 2½″ to either side to complete the chimney section. Press the seams toward the darker fabrics.

Assemble the chimney section.

**3.** Piece the roof section. Sew 2 half-square triangles using the 2 background squares 2½″ × 2½″ and 2 roof squares 2½″ × 2½″. Sew a dark square 2½″ × 2½″ to each end of a background rectangle

2½″ × 3½″. Trim the seams and press them toward the roof fabric. You now have 3 pieced roof components and 1 roof rectangle. Sew them together as shown.

Assemble the roof.

**4.** Piece the door section. Sew the 1½″ × 2½″ window and the 2½″ × 3½″ door to either side of the 1½″ × 2½″ wall piece. Press the seams toward the darker fabric. Sew 2 wall pieces 1½″ × 5½″ to the sides of this unit, and then add the 1½″ × 4½″ wall piece to the top. Press the seams toward the longest fabric pieces.

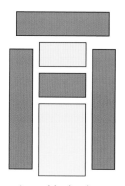

Assemble the door.

**5.** Piece the window section. Sew the window squares to either side of the 1½″ × 1½″ wall squares, pressing the seams toward the darker fabric. Add the 1½″ × 3½″ walls and the 1½″ × 5½″ top and bottom walls in the same manner

as Step 4, pressing the seams toward the longest fabric pieces.

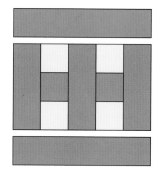

Assemble the window.

**6.** Add the 1½″ × 5½″ top and 1½″ × 6½″ left side background strips to the window section. Press the seams toward the background

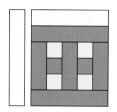

Complete the window section.

**7.** Sew the door and window sections together, and press the seam toward the background.

**8.** Sew the roof onto the unit from Step 7. Press the seam toward the door and window.

**9.** Sew the chimneys to the top of the roof, and press the seam toward the chimneys.

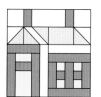 

School House block alternate colorways

# Four Schools Wallhanging

**FINISHED WALLHANGING: 28″ × 28″**

Pieced by Heidi Uselmann,
quilted by Janet McWorkman

*This wallhanging is a great gift for a teacher. You could also add large borders to the School House blocks and sew them together to make a baby quilt. The fabric requirements listed for the project are to make four identical houses; however, if you'd prefer to make each house look different (as in the sample), you can use scraps.*

## Materials

Background and first inner border:
½ yard

House walls: ⅜ yard

Roofs and center cornerstone:
¼ yard

Windows and door: ⅛ yard

Chimneys and second inner
border: ¼ yard

Floral outer border: ½ yard

Backing: ⅞ yard

Batting: 30″ × 30″

Binding: ¼ yard

## Cutting

Makes 1 wallhanging.

| FOR | CUT | SIZE |
|---|---|---|
| Background, sashing, and first inner border | 16 | 2½″ × 2½″ |
| | 4 | 2½″ × 3½″ |
| | 4 | 2½″ × 4½″ |
| | 4 | 1½″ × 5½″ |
| | 4 | 1½″ × 6½″ |
| | 4 | 1½″ × 10½″ |
| | 2 | 1″ × 21½″ |
| | 2 | 1″ × 22½″ |
| House walls | 16 | 1½″ × 5½″ |
| | 4 | 1½″ × 4½″ |
| | 12 | 1½″ × 3½″ |
| | 4 | 1½″ × 2½″ |
| | 8 | 1½″ × 1½″ |

*Cutting continued*

| FOR | CUT | SIZE |
|---|---|---|
| Roofs and center cornerstone | 16 | 2½″ × 2½″ |
| | 4 | 2½″ × 3½″ |
| | 1 | 1½″ × 1½″ |
| Windows and doors | 16 | 1½″ × 1½″ |
| | 4 | 1½″ × 2½″ |
| | 4 | 2½″ × 3½″ |
| Chimneys and second inner border | 8 | 1½″ × 2½″ |
| | 2 | 1″ × 22½″ |
| | 2 | 1″ × 23½″ |
| Outer border | 2 | 3″ × 23½″ |
| | 2 | 3″ × 28½″ |
| Binding | 2 | 2¼″ × WOF |

# Finish the Wallhanging

*For detailed instructions on sashing and cornerstones, making a quilt sandwich, quilting, and binding, refer to Quiltmaking Basics (page 13).*

## Make the Quilt Top

*Four Schools* wallhanging assembly

**1.** Make 4 blocks as instructed in School House Block (page 47). Press the blocks and square them up. They should measure 10½″ × 10½″ square.

**2.** Sew 2 School House blocks to either side of a sashing piece 1½″ × 10½″. Repeat with the other 2 School House blocks. Press the seams toward the sashing.

**3.** Sew 2 sashing pieces 1½″ × 10½″ to either side of the cornerstone square 1½″ × 1½″. Press the seams toward the sashing.

**4.** Sew the sashing strip from Step 3 between the 2 rows of School House blocks from Step 2, matching the seams at the cornerstone. Press the seams toward the sashing.

## BORDERS

**1.** Sew the first inner borders to the sides of the quilt top and press the seams toward the border strips. Then sew the top and bottom first inner border strips to the quilt top and press the seams toward the borders.

**2.** Repeat Step 1 to attach the second inner borders.

**3.** Repeat Step 1 to attach the outer borders.

## BACKING

Cut the backing 30″ × 30″.

## Sandwich, Quilt, and Bind

**1.** Make a quilt sandwich with the backing, batting, and top.

**2.** Quilt, using the method of your choice.

**3.** Bind the wallhanging.

**4.** Label and love.

Many quilters are stuck designing exclusively with straight lines because sewing curves seems too scary. Don't be one of those quilters! This chapter will teach you a method that will make you feel like you can take on any block with curves. You will also learn a foolproof appliqué method.

The Drunkard's Path has a rich history. Its name probably came from its connection to the Women's Christian Temperance Union of 1892. There are many placement variations for this versatile block, which is enjoying popularity in the modern quilting revival. Entire quilt books feature only Drunkard's Path block variations.

# DRUNKARD'S PATH BLOCK

Drunkard's Path block

## Materials

Choose 4 fabrics: 2 lights and 2 darks. (Minimum sizes listed below.)

Light 1: 7″ × 11″

Light 2: 7″ × 11″

Dark 1: 7″ × 11″

Dark 2: 7″ × 11″

## Cutting

Makes 1 block.

| FROM | CUT | USING |
|------|-----|-------|
| Light 1 | 4 | Template A |
| Light 2 | 4 | |
| Light 1 | 4 | Template B |
| Light 2 | 4 | |
| Dark 1 | 4 | Template A |
| Dark 2 | 4 | |
| Dark 1 | 4 | Template B |
| Dark 2 | 4 | |

## Make the Block

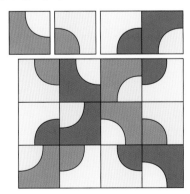

Drunkard's Path block assembly

*Use Drunkard's Path patterns A and B (pullout page P1) to make templates. For instructions on making a template, refer to Key Techniques: Making a Template (page 31).*

**1.** Make 16 Drunkard's Path blocks, referring to Key Technique: Curved Piecing (page 51).

**2.** Following the block assembly diagram, arrange 4 rows of 4 blocks to your liking.

**3.** Sew the blocks into rows and then sew together the rows, pressing the seams open to reduce bulk.

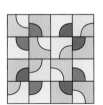 

Drunkard's Path block alternate colorways

# KEY TECHNIQUE: Curved Piecing

*Follow this tutorial for piecing the curve in a Drunkard's Path block. Use the same method to sew smooth curves elsewhere. Practice on scraps before making the block for your sampler quilt.*

**1.** Pair up all A and B pieces, making sure each pair has both a light and a dark fabric.

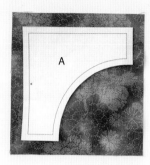

**2.** Cut an A and a B piece. Fold and crease each fabric piece in half at the curved edge to mark the center point.

**3.** Pin an A and B pair at that crease, right sides together.

**4.** Clip the inside curve of piece A about every ½˝. Pin both the beginning and the ending of the curved seamline.

**5.** With piece A on top, slowly stitch the curved seam, gently adjusting the top piece to avoid puckers. Remove the pins as you approach them.

**6.** Press the seam toward piece A.

# HEARTS AND GIZZARDS BLOCK

*The Quilter's Primer* version of the Hearts and Gizzards block is a fun, little block with only a small amount of appliqué. The curved raw edges are turned under with the help of a heat-resistant template material and starch. This starch technique will be used for all the alphabet letters in the sampler quilt. Practice here on a little heart, so you will have a leg up later for the appliqué work.

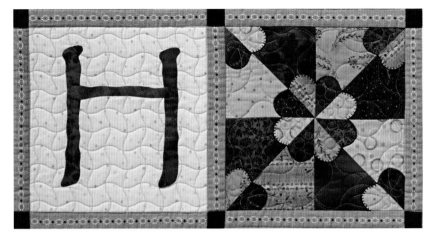

Hearts and Gizzards block

## Materials

Choose 8 fabrics: 4 lights and 4 darks. (Minimum sizes listed below.)

4 lights: 7″ × 10″ of each

4 darks: 7″ × 10″ of each

## Cutting

Makes 1 block.

| FROM | CUT | SIZE |
|---|---|---|
| Each of 4 lights | 1 | 6″ × 6″ for a total of 4 squares |
| | 1 | 3″ × 6″ for a total of 4 rectangles |
| Each of 4 darks | 1 | 6″ × 6″ for a total of 4 squares |
| | 1 | 3″ × 6″ for a total of 4 rectangles |

## Make the Block

*Use the Hearts and Gizzards patterns (pullout page P1) to make templates. For detailed instructions, refer to: Key Technique: Making a Template (page 31); Key Technique: Half-Square Triangles (page 28); and Key Technique: Starch-Turned Appliqué (page 54).*

Hearts and Gizzards block assembly

## tip

Making two templates will enable you to press one appliqué heart while another is cooling.

**1.** Make 4 half-square triangles with the light and dark squares. Trim to measure exactly 5½″ × 5½″.

**2.** Pair up a small light rectangle with a small dark rectangle. Stitch them together along their long sides and press the seam open. Make 8.

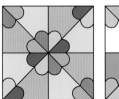 

Hearts and Gizzards block alternate colorways

**3.** Using the Hearts and Gizzards template and a No. 2 pencil, draw 2 hearts on the wrong side of each unit pieced in Step 2. Watch the direction of the template on the fabric. You need a pair of *opposite* hearts from each strip set. Cut out all 8 hearts ¼″ outside the drawn line.

**4.** Using diluted starch and a hot, dry iron, fold in the curved seam allowances for all the hearts around the template. Note that the seam allowance is only turned for the top curve; the sides of the heart will be caught in the seam allowance when you sew together the 4 units.

**5.** Remove the template and use temporary fabric glue dots to affix the heart onto the assembled background square.

**6.** Appliqué 2 hearts to each half-square triangle by hand or machine. The Hearts and Gizzards block in *The Quilter's Primer* was machine appliquéd using black Aurifil 40-weight thread and a blanket stitch.

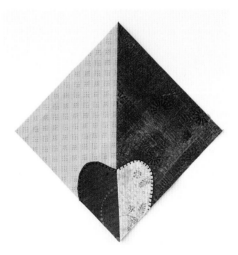

**7.** Sew the 4 squares together to complete the block. Press the seams open to reduce bulk.

There are many ways to appliqué, and each has it star qualities and challenges. All projects in this book use starch-turned appliqué.

## Getting Started

### Supplies

- Several sheets of heat-resistant plastic (such as Mylar or Templar)
- Roxanne Glue-Baste-It
- Liquid starch
- Small bottle with a tight lid
- Fine-point permanent marker (such as a Sharpie Ultra Fine Point Permanent Marker)
- No. 2 pencil
- Small brush

Starch-turned appliqué tools

### Basic Steps

- Make and label the templates.
- Trace template shapes onto the fabric.
- Cut out fabric shapes, adding a ¼″ seam allowance.
- Turn under ¼″ seam allowance.
- Remove templates.
- Affix the appliqué pieces to the background.
- Sew the appliqués to the background.

## Make and Label Templates

**1.** Place a template sheet over the pattern and trace the templates you will use. A thin Sharpie works well and doesn't smudge. Label each template.

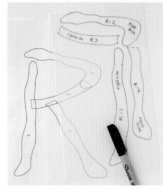

Make templates and label on the right side.

### tip

Cut smooth curves. Any little poky edge can be seen on the finished appliqué. Use an emery board or nail file to smooth the template before tracing.

**2.** Cut out the templates exactly on the traced line. (Do not add a seam allowance to the template.)

## Trace Shape onto Fabric

**1.** Select the fabric for your appliqué.

**2.** Place the template so the wrong side of both the template and the fabric is facing you.

**3.** Trace the template using a No. 2 pencil or a fabric marking pen.

Draw on the fabric's wrong side following the template's exact shape.

## Cut Out Fabric Shape

**1.** Cut out the fabric, adding a scant ¼″ seam allowance. Just eyeball it—this does not have to be exact.

**2.** If your shape has inside curves, clip the seam allowance every ¼″ from the cut edge almost to your drawn lines.

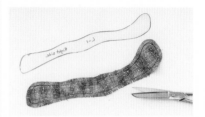

Cut out the fabric and clip the inside curves.

### Turn Under ¼″ Seam Allowance

**1.** In a small bottle with a tight lid, mix 1 part starch to 3 parts water. The mixture lasts about a week.

**2.** Use a small brush to dampen a short section of the seam allowance with the diluted starch.

**3.** Set your iron to high but do not use steam. Press the seam allowance over the template edge. Go slowly and don't burn your fingers. This will take practice. Look for videos online showing this technique.

With a hot, dry iron, press the seam allowance onto the template material.

**4.** At outside curves, add more diluted starch and fold the seam allowance around the curve, pleating the inside edge. Press flat.

**5.** Keep working around the template, adding more diluted starch as needed. An inside corner with clipped edges will easily iron flat.

Clip inside corners to ease turning the seam allowance.

### Remove the Template

**1.** Allow the pressed appliqué piece to cool completely.

**2.** Gently run a fingernail under the seam allowance adhered to the template to loosen it. On outside corners, pinch the fabric as you remove the template.

When cool, pop out the template.

**3.** After the appliqué piece is free from the template, press it with a dry iron one last time to flatten it. This will make it easier to sew down.

### Glue Pieces to Background

**1.** Place your appliqué on the background fabric.

**2.** Use tiny dots of Roxanne Glue-Baste-It or diluted school glue to affix the appliqué.

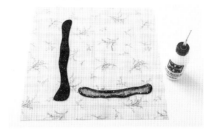

**3.** If you come to an intersection of 2 appliqué pieces, tuck a raw edge under a finished edge.

Tuck in raw edges before gluing them down.

### Sew Appliqué to Background

You can sew down your appliqués by hand or machine.

#### Hand Sewing

▪ If you don't want your stitching to show, use very thin thread that is the same color as the appliqué piece. A 50-weight silk thread works wonderfully and nearly disappears into the fabric. Run a hand stitch behind the background and bring the thread to the surface only for tiny "bites" of the appliqué.

▪ Or use a blanket stitch. Choose a matching or contrasting thread.

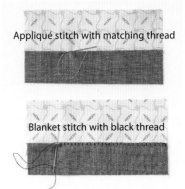

Appliqué stitch with matching thread

Blanket stitch with black thread

### Machine Sewing

Check the stitches available on your machine; you may have several that would work nicely for appliqué. I like a blanket stitch with a short stitch length and Aurifil thread (40 or 50 weight) in a color that matches the appliqué piece. You can also use a straight stitch close to the edge.

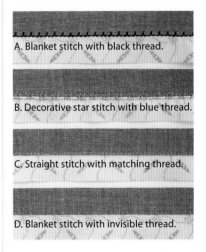

A. Blanket stitch with black thread.

B. Decorative star stitch with blue thread.

C. Straight stitch with matching thread.

D. Blanket stitch with invisible thread.

### tip

Practice machine appliqué on a double thickness of scrap fabric. Set tensions, stitch width, and length until you're happy with the results. Record the settings for future reference.

# ORANGE PEEL BLOCK

Orange Peel block

The Orange Peel block has a very graphic quality. It is enjoying a revival with modern quilters who pair gigantic peels of bright colors with low-volume neutrals.

## Materials

Choose 4 fabrics: 2 darks for the background and 2 medium lights for the peels. (Minimum sizes listed below.)

A dark background: 7″ × 13″

B dark background: 7″ × 13″

A medium-light peel: 7″ × 13″

B medium-light peel: 7″ × 13″

## Cutting

*Use the Orange Peel pattern (pullout page P1) to make a template. For detailed instructions, refer to Key Technique: Make a Template (page 31).*

Makes 1 block.

| FROM | CUT | SIZE |
|---|---|---|
| A dark background | 8 | 3″ × 3″ |
| B dark background | 8 | 3″ × 3″ |
| A medium-light peel | 8 | Orange Peel template |
| B medium-light peel | 8 | Orange Peel template |

## Make the Block

*For detailed instructions, refer to Key Technique: Make a Nine-Patch (page 31) and Key Technique: Starch-Turned Appliqué (page 54).*

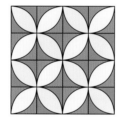

Orange Peel block assembly

**1.** Sew together the checkerboard background into Four-Patch blocks using the 2 dark fabrics. Press the seams toward the darker fabric.

**2.** Using the Orange Peel template, draw 16 peels on the wrong side of the medium-light fabric. Cut them out with a ¼″ seam allowance.

**3.** Using the template, starch, and a hot iron, fold in the seam allowances around each of the 16 peels. Make the points nice and sharp by folding down the end and then each side.

With starch and a hot iron, turn under the raw edges.

**4.** Remove the template material and place the peels on the background. Use dots of fabric glue to temporarily attach the peels. Be sure to leave ¼″ seam allowance on the outside edges of the pieced Four-Patch blocks.

**5.** Using either machine or hand appliqué, sew all the peels to the 4 background Four-Patch blocks.

**6.** Sew each pair of blocks together, pressing the seams in opposite directions before sewing the rows together. Give the block a final gentle pressing.

Orange Peel block alternate colorways

# FALLING LEAVES QUILT

**FINISHED QUILT:** $62'' \times 72''$

Pieced by Pamela Wicks,
quilted by Amanda Leins

## Materials

| | LAP, 62″ × 72″, 20 BLOCKS | DOUBLE, 72″ × 82″, 30 BLOCKS | QUEEN, 82″ × 92″, 42 BLOCKS |
|---|---|---|---|
| Peels | ¼ yard of 5 different lights | ¼ yard of 7 different lights | ¼ yard of 9 different lights |
| Navy block background | 2½ yards | 3¼ yards | 4½ yards |
| Brown block background | 2½ yards | 3¼ yards | 4½ yards |
| First navy border | 1 yard | 1¼ yards | 1½ yards |
| Second brown border | 1¼ yards | 1½ yards | 1¾ yards |
| Backing | 3⅝ yards | 4¾ yards | 7 yards |
| Batting | Twin size | Double size | Queen size |
| Binding | ½ yard | ⅝ yard | ¾ yard |

## Cutting

Make a template with the Falling Leaves pattern (pullout page P1). For detailed instructions on making a template, refer to Key Technique: Make a Template (page 31).

WOF = width of fabric

| FOR | CUT | | | SIZE |
|---|---|---|---|---|
| | Lap | Double | Queen | |
| Lights | 98 | 138 | 186 | Falling Leaves template |
| Navy background | 40 | 60 | 84 | 5½″ × 5½″ |
| Brown background | 40 | 60 | 84 | 5½″ × 5½″ |
| First navy border | 5 | 6 | 7 | 5½″ × WOF |
| Second brown border | 7 | 8 | 9 | 5½″ × WOF |

# Make the Blocks

*For detailed instructions on making the blocks for this quilt, refer to Orange Peel Block (page 56).*

**1.** Sew together sets of 4 navy and brown squares into Four-Patch blocks to make the checkerboard background for your quilt size. Press the seams toward the darker fabric.

Alternate navy and brown squares when sewing together the background.

**2.** Using the Falling Leaves template, trace leaves on the wrong side of the light fabric, allowing a ¼″ seam allowance. Refer to the cutting chart to see how many you need for your quilt size. Cut out all the leaves ¼″ outside the drawn line.

**3.** Using the template, turn under all the leaf edges with the help of diluted starch and an iron.

**4.** Machine or hand appliqué the leaves to the background checkerboard blocks. Be careful to leave ¼″ seam allowance on the outside block edges when you place the peels.

*Falling Leaves* leaf placement

**5.** Sew the blocks together into rows. Press the seams in each row in opposite directions.

**6.** Sew together the rows. Press the seams to one side.

**7.** Sew the border strips together end to end and cut to the size for your quilt.

| | | LAP | DOUBLE | QUEEN |
|---|---|---|---|---|
| First border | Sides | 5½″ × 50½″ | 5½″ × 60½″ | 5½″ × 70½″ |
| | Top and bottom | 5½″ × 50½″ | 5½″ × 60½″ | 5½″ × 70½″ |
| Second border | Sides | 6½″ × 60½″ | 6½″ × 70½″ | 6½″ × 80½″ |
| | Top and bottom | 6½″ × 72½″ | 6½″ × 82½″ | 6½″ × 92½″ |

**8.** Add the first border to the sides; then add the top and bottom borders. Press the seams toward the borders.

**9.** Repeat Step 8 for the second borders.

**10.** Add the remaining leaf appliqués. It is helpful to sketch where you want to place the leaves for the alternate larger sizes.

# Finish the Quilt

*For detailed instructions on making a quilt sandwich, quilting, and binding, refer to Quiltmaking Basics (page 13).*

*Falling Leaves* quilt assembly

## Sandwich, Quilt, and Bind

**1.** Make a quilt sandwich with the backing, batting, and top.

**2.** Quilt, using the method of your choice.

**3.** Bind the quilt.

**4.** Label and love.

## JAPANESE FAN BLOCK

This chapter continues to build on your knowledge of paper piecing and appliqué, while learning to work with circles and points.

The Japanese Fan block was often constructed of in red and white silk to reflect the Japanese flag. This version is both effective and surprisingly easy.

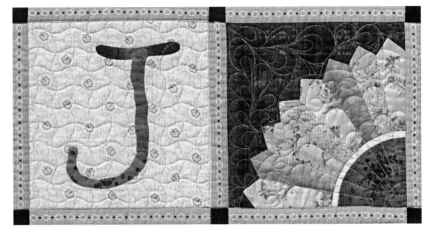

Japanese Fan block

### Materials

The Quilter's Primer *uses four fabrics for the eight fan blades. Consider a stripe for the fan blades or fussy cutting the fan center.*

Choose a range of fabrics: a dark for the background, 4 medium scraps for the fan blades, and both a light and medium dark for the fan center. (Minimum sizes listed below.)

Dark background fabric: 11″ × 11″

Medium fan blade 1: 4″ × 8″

Medium fan blade 2: 4″ × 8″

Medium fan blade 3: 4″ × 8″

Medium fan blade 4: 4″ × 8″

Medium-dark center: 5″ × 5″

Light center ring: 6″ × 6″

### Cutting

Makes 1 block.

| FROM | CUT | SIZE |
|---|---|---|
| Dark | 1 | 10½″ × 10½″ |
| Mediums 1–4 | 2 from each fabric | Template A |
| Light | 1 | Template B |
| Medium dark | 1 | Template C |

## Make the Block

*Use Japanese Fan patterns A, B, and C (pullout page P2) to make templates. For detailed instructions, refer to Key Technique: Making a Template (page 31) and Key Technique: Starch-Backed Appliqué (page 54).*

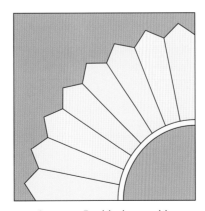

Japanese Fan block assembly

**1.** Cut 8 fan blades using template A. Fold all the fan blades in half lengthwise, right sides together. Chain stitch them, sewing the top flat edge with a scant ¼″ seam. Clip the corner.

**2.** Finger-press the seam open and turn it inside out. Using a turning tool of your choice (my favorite is a Phillips screwdriver) gently push out the fan blade point. Repeat for all the fan blades. Press them flat, centering the point.

**3.** Arrange the fan blades to your liking. Stitch the pairs together, starting at the narrow end, sew to the pressed points, and backstitch about ½". Press the seams open.

**4.** Fold the background square in half diagonally and press the fold. Repeat for the opposite diagonal. Place the fan blades on the background square, using the pressed lines as guides. Pin or glue the blades to the background.

**5.** Using templates B and C, cut out the center ring and center.

**6.** Turn under the ¼" seam allowance on both quarter-circles.

**7.** Hand or machine appliqué the center ring B over the blade edges, then the center C on top of B.

Japanese Fan block alternate colorways

# UNION STAR BLOCK

Union Star block

The five-pointed Union Star block evokes the American flag and is beloved by patriotic quilters. This version centers the star inside a large circle. The star is paper pieced, and the outside circle is reverse appliquéd.

## Materials

Choose 4 fabrics: 1 dark background, 1 light circle, 1 medium for the star points, and 1 dark for the star center. (Minimum sizes listed below.)

Dark background: 11″ × 11″

Light circle: 9″ × 16″

Medium star points: 7″ × 13″

Dark star center: 4″ × 4″

## Cutting

Makes 1 block.

| FROM | CUT | SIZE |
|---|---|---|
| Dark background | 1 | 11″ × 11″ |
| Light center circle | 5 | 4″ × 5″ |
| Medium star points | 5 | 3″ × 4″ |
| Dark star center | 1 | 4″ × 4″ |

# Make the Block

*Use the Union Star foundation patterns (pullout page P2). For detailed instructions, refer to Key Technique: Foundation Paper Piecing (page 38).*

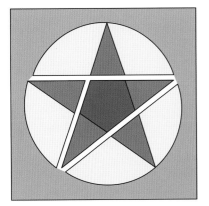

Union Star center assembly

**1.** Trace or photocopy each of the 4 Union Star foundation patterns, A, A-reversed, B, and C.

**2.** Paper piece the star sections in numerical order. Press each section on the fabric side.

**3.** Trim the sections, using the paper as a guide; your seam allowance will then be exactly ¼″.

**4.** Arrange all 4 sections as shown in the center assembly diagram, carefully placing the 2 foundation patterns that are mirror images, making sure the seamlines match exactly. Sew together the 4 sections.

**5.** Remove the paper foundation carefully and press.

**6.** Fold the background square on the diagonal twice to find the a center point. Using a compass and starting at the center point, draw a 7½″-diameter circle. Cut out this center circle.

Cut out circle.

**7.** Use the compass to draw a 4″-radius quarter-circle on the heat-resistant template sheet. Cut an outside arc piece to use as a pressing template.

**8.** Clip the curve every ½″. Turn under the center circle seam allowance and press, using the pressing template for a smooth pressed edge. Refer to Key Technique: Starch-Turned Appliqué (page 54).

Use a pressing template to help turn back ¼″ seam allowance.

**9.** Fold the prepared background fabric in half and press to mark the middle point. Place it facedown and line up a star point, also facedown, with the pressed line. Affix the star to the background with pins or fabric glue.

Back of Union Star, finished with blanket stitch applique

**10.** Appliqué the background to the star either by hand or machine.

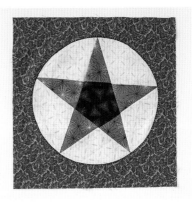

Finished Union Star block

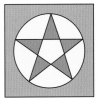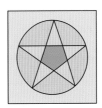

Union Star block alternate colorways

The Mariner's Compass block is one of the oldest quilt blocks known. It goes by many names, including Sunburst, Sunrise, and Compass Rose. We'll make a relatively easy compass block with eight paper-pieced rays and an appliquéd center medallion. Finally the entire compass is reverse appliquéd onto a square to complete the block. The version in *The Quilter's Primer* has more points and two center rings.

# MARINER'S COMPASS BLOCK

Mariner's Compass block

## Materials

Choose 5 fabrics. (Minimum sizes listed below.)

Light background: 17″ × 22″

Dark wide ray: 8″ × 12″

Medium-dark skinny ray: 6″ × 12″

Light center triangles: 6″ × 11″

Medium-light center circle: 5″ × 5″

## Cutting

Makes 1 block.

| FOR | CUT | SIZE |
|---|---|---|
| Background | 1 | 10½″ × 10½″ |
| | 8 | 5″ × 5″ |
| Dark wide ray | 4 | 4″ × 6″ |
| Medium-dark skinny ray | 4 | 3″ × 6″ |
| Center triangles | 8 | 2½″ × 2½″ |
| Medium-light center circle | 1 | 4″ × 4″ |

*tip*

The center circle is a great place to showcase a fussy-cut motif such as a ship, flower, or star.

## Make the Block

*Use the Mariner's Compass A, B, C, and center patterns (pullout page P1). Make a template with the center pattern. For detailed instructions, refer to Key Technique: Make a Template; Key Technique: Foundation Paper Piecing (page 38); and Key Technique: Starch-Turned Appliqué (page 54).*

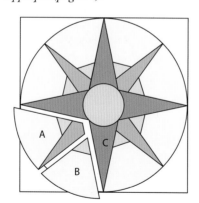

Mariner's Compass block assembly

**1.** Trace or photocopy the Mariner's Compass wedge patterns A and B; you will need 4 copies. Mark each section with the fabric you intend to place there.

**2.** Look at how the foundation pattern pieces come together. The longest point C is a pattern to cut the dark rays.

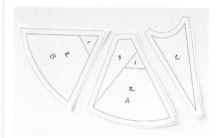

Mariner's Compass foundation patterns

**3.** Paper piece the A and B sections of the Mariner's Compass.

Paper piece the compass sections, adding the long star point as shown.

**4.** Sew together each set of A and B sections for a quarter-wedge; then add the longest star point C.

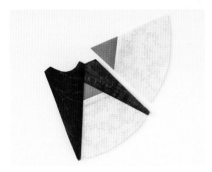

Sew together a complete quarter-section of the compass.

**5.** Repeat Steps 3 and 4 for all remaining compass sections

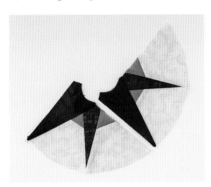

Repeat for all remaining compass sections.

**6.** Using the center circle template and adding a scant ¼″ seam allowance, cut the center circle fabric. This is a great place to fussy cut a motif, if desired.

Cut fabric for the center circle.

**7.** Using a hot, dry iron and a bit of starch, turn under the ¼″ seam allowance around the center circle.

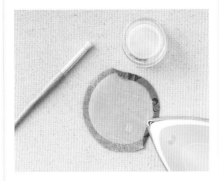

**8.** Affix the center circle on the pieced compass with pins or fabric glue. Hand or machine appliqué the circle in place.

**9.** Fold the 11″ × 11″ background square in half twice and press to mark the center point. Starting at the center and using a compass set at 4¼″ radius, draw a 9½″-diameter circle on the wrong side of the background fabric.

**10.** Cut out the center on the drawn line. This includes a ¼″ seam allowance.

**11.** Use the compass to draw a 5″-radius quarter-circle on the heat-resistant template sheet. Cut an outside arc piece to use as a pressing template to help smoothly turn under the ¼″ seam allowance. See Union Star Block, Make the Block, Step 8 photo (page 61).

**12.** Using pins or fabric glue, secure the compass to the background square, lining up the compass on the crease.

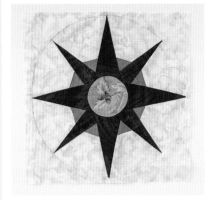

Mariner's Compass ready to be appliquéd

**13.** Hand or machine appliqué the background square to the compass. Press and trim to an exact 10½″ × 10½″ square

Mariner's Compass block alternate colorways

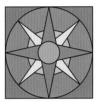

# BUTTERFLY FANS QUILT

**FINISHED QUILT:** *57″ × 71″*

Pieced by Janet McWorkman,
quilted by Amanda Leins

## Materials

|  | LAP<br>57″ × 71″ | TWIN<br>71″ × 85″ |
|---|---|---|
| **Block info** | | |
| Full blocks | 20 appliquéd,<br>12 solid | 30 appliquéd,<br>20 solid |
| Half-blocks | 14 | 18 |
| Corner blocks | 4 | 4 |
| **Yardage** | | |
| Block background | 4 yards | 5¾ yards |
| Fan blades | ½ yard each of<br>5 fabrics | ¾ yard each of<br>5 fabrics |
| Fan centers | ¼ yard | ⅜ yard |
| Backing | 3½ yards | 5 yards |
| Batting | Twin size | Twin size |
| Binding | ⅝ yard | ¾ yard |

## Cutting

*WOF = width of fabric*

| FOR | CUT | | SIZE | SUBCUT |
|---|---|---|---|---|
| | Lap | Twin | | |
| Background | 32 | 50 | Full blocks,<br>10½″ × 10½″ | — |
| | 4 | 5 | Half-blocks,<br>15½″ × 15½″ | Subcut diagonally<br>twice. |
| | 2 | 2 | Corner blocks,<br>8″ × 8″ | Subcut diagonally<br>once. |
| Fan blades | 20 each of 5 fabrics for a<br>total of 100 blades | 30 each of 5 fabrics for a<br>total of 150 blades | Template A | — |
| Fan center | 20 | 30 | Template B | — |
| Binding | 7 strips | 9 strips | 2¼″ × WOF | — |

# Make the Quilt Top

*For detailed instructions, refer to Japanese Fan Block (page 59). Note that this version of the block has five blades (instead of eight) and one center quarter-circle (instead of two). Make templates from Butterfly Fans patterns A and B (pullout page P2).*

**1.** Select 5 fan blades for each block. Sew the blades following Japanese Fan Block, Steps 1 and 2 (page 59).

**2.** With the help of template center B, turn under the ¼″ seam allowance on the curved edge of all the fan quarter-circle centers.

**3.** Affix the fan blades and the quarter-circle to the background square with pins or fabric glue.

**4.** Hand or machine appliqué the fan section and a fan center to the background square.

**5.** Arrange the blocks to your liking. The lap quilt size is illustrated. The twin-size quilt will have one more row and column.

**6.** Add the alternate blank blocks, the half-blocks along the edges, and the corner blocks.

**7.** Sew the blocks together in diagonal rows. Press the seams in each row to one side, and press the next row to the opposite side.

**9.** Sew the rows together and press.

# Finish the Quilt

*For detailed instructions on making a quilt sandwich, quilting, and binding, refer to Quiltmaking Basics (page 13).*

## Backing

Piece the backing for the quilt as needed. Trim for lap-size to 61″ × 75″ or for twin-size to 75″ × 89″.

## Sandwich, Quilt, and Bind

**1.** Make a quilt sandwich with the backing, batting, and top.

**2.** Quilt, using the method of your choice.

**3.** Bind the quilt.

**4.** Label and love.

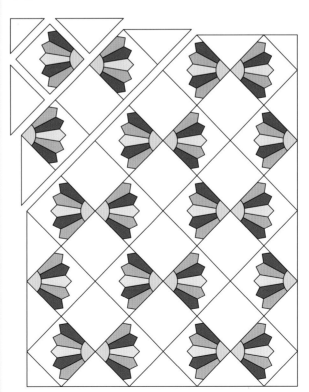

*Butterfly Fans* quilt assembly

There are many ways to piece blocks, and quilters develop personal preferences. Sometimes a pattern dictates what will be the easiest method to get the best results. Sometimes the fabric will lead you in a particular direction. Make the blocks in this chapter to solidify your skills with foundation piecing, learn English paper piecing, and find out what a *yo-yo* is in the quilting world, all while using up some scraps.

Need a break from measurements, templates, and precision? A crazy quilt is the answer. These create-as-you-go quilts free you up to improvise. Our quilting great-grandmothers saved bits of dress fabric, silk, velvet, and ribbons—and then they just winged it, sometimes adding gorgeous embroidery to enhance the fabric. We'll use a square foundation pattern for this block, though there are many other approaches.

## CRAZY QUILT BLOCK

Crazy Quilt block

### Materials

Choose 4–6 different fabric strips each about 4″ × 15″ to start. Fabric requirements for a crazy quilt are quite flexible.

*tip*

Try your hand at drawing a unique pattern for a couple of the 5½″ × 5½″ blocks. Just draw random lines across the foundation that somewhat adhere to a Log Cabin type of construction. Start with a small triangle or hexagon in the center for a different Crazy Quilt block.

## Make the Block

*Use the Crazy Quilt foundation pattern (pullout page P2). For detailed instructions, refer to Key Technique: Foundation Paper Piecing (page 38). You will need an Add-A-Quarter ruler to make this block.*

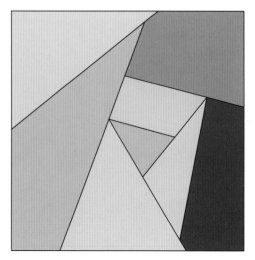

Crazy Quilt block assembly

**1.** Photocopy or trace 4 copies of the Crazy Quilt foundation pattern.

Gather many scraps of fabric for the Crazy Quilt block.

**2.** Select a fabric for piece 1 on the paper foundation and pin in place, allowing for ¼″ seam allowance. Align the second fabric with the first piece.

Start in the middle and line up the first and second fabrics.

**3.** Sew together the 2 fabrics along the seamline between spaces 1 and 2, using a stitch length of 1 mm or 24 stitches per inch.

Do not sew across the seamlines on the paper foundation.

**4.** Finger-press the fabric open and use an Add-a-Quarter ruler to trim the seam.

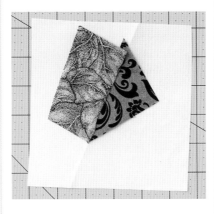

**5.** Add the next fabric. Trim the fabric on the seam allowance line. Do not cut the paper.

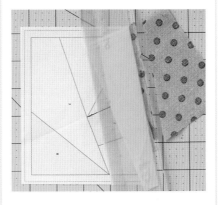

**6.** Continue adding fabrics, in numerical order, until the block is completely covered.

**7.** Press the block on the fabric side and trim it on the outside line

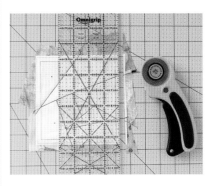

**8.** Repeat Steps 2–7 to make 3 more sections. Remove the paper foundation.

Make 4 sections.

**9.** Sew all 4 sections into a square 10½″ × 10½″. Embellish with embroidery if desired.

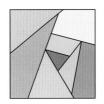

Crazy Quilt block alternate colorways

Everyone has seen a quilt made with this pattern. It is ubiquitous in American and English culture. It is also enjoying a revival within the modern quilting community, where neutrals and bold solids are often showcased. While larger hexagons, like those in the Inner City block, can be machine stitched using set-in seams, smaller hexagons are more easily tackled with the English paper piecing method.

# GRANDMOTHER'S FLOWER GARDEN BLOCK

Grandmother's Flower Garden block

## Materials

Choose 7 fabrics: 4 for flower petals, 2 for flower centers, and 1 for the background.

This is the time to dig into the scraps you've accumulated making blocks. You need 46 pieces about 3″ × 3″. Go rogue and make your own design, or copy the block in *The Quilter's Primer.*

## *tip*

There are many ways hexagons can be set, forming very different patterns. Get inspiration by searching the Internet for hexagon quilts.

## Cutting

*Use the Grandmother's Flower Garden pattern (pullout page P1) to make a template.*

1. From card stock, cut 46 hexagons, using the Grandmother's Flower Garden template. I cut mine out of throwaway postcards that come in magazines. Or purchase precut 1″ finished-size hexagon templates.

2. Draw 46 hexagons on the back of the fabric pieces, allowing for at least ¼″ seam allowance around each. *To make the flower design as shown, you need 22 background hexagons, 6 petals for 3 of the flowers, and 2 petals for the partial flower.*

3. Cut out the hexagons, adding a generous ¼″ seam allowance all around. I sometimes add nearly ½″.

## Make the Block

*Please read through all directions before beginning; the construction method is very different from those used in previous blocks.*

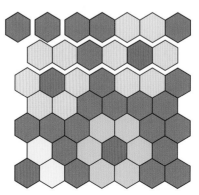

Grandmother's Flower Garden block assembly

1. Dab a bit of glue to the wrong side of a fabric hexagon and center a card stock template in place.

2. Turn under the seam allowance and hand stitch in place. Use a running stitch to miter the corners as you go, being careful not to catch the card stock. It may look difficult, but after doing it a couple of times, it becomes very easy. Make 46.

Finger-press and fold the corners so they lie flat.

**3.** Press all the turned hexagons on the fabric side.

**4.** Arrange the hexagons as shown in the assembly diagram, forming rows and columns.

**5.** Sew together 2 hexagon units by hand, using a whipstitch or a blind stitch. Try to not to catch the paper as you sew.

*tip*

This is a wonderful take-along project for long car rides, airplane trips, or doctor office visits.

**6.** Sew together all the hexagons in the same manner as in Step 5, paying attention to the number of hexagons in each row. It's easy to get lost!

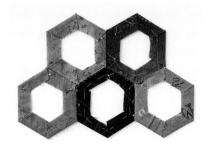

The back of several hexagons sewn together

**7.** When all 46 hexagons are sewn together, pop out the paper foundations and press the block.

**8.** Trim the block using a 10½″ × 10½″ square ruler.

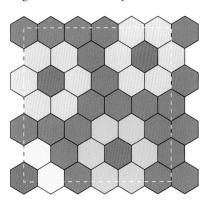

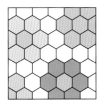 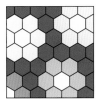

Grandmother's Flower Garden block alternate colorways

# TALL TREE BLOCK

Tall Tree block

I'm going to come clean. … The original block in the quilt challenged me almost to the breaking point. I actually started and restarted it many times. I have since changed the pattern and instructions for the block to make it somewhat easier, but I won't kid you … it is a challenge. And I think you can do it.

## Materials

*The Quilter's Primer* uses about 6 different greens for the trees, but here we use just 1 dark and 1 light. (Minimum sizes listed at right.)

Background fabric: 10″ × 11″

Dark tree fabric: 12″ × 14″

Light tree fabric: 11″ × 12″

Trunk fabric: 3″ × 3″

Border: 6″ × 12″

Makes 1 block.

| FOR | CUT | SIZE | SUBCUT |
|---|---|---|---|
| Background | 1 | 7″ × 9½″ | Subcut 1 using background I pattern and 1 reversed. |
| | 2 | 2″ × 4″ | — |
| Dark tree | 10 | 2½″ × 3½″ | Subcut once on the diagonal to yield 20 triangles. |
| | 5 | 2½″ × 2½″ | — |
| Light tree | 10 | 2½″ × 3½″ | Subcut once on the diagonal to yield 20 triangles. |
| Trunk | 1 | 2″ × 2½″ | — |
| Border | 2 | 1¼″ × 9″ | — |
| | 2 | 1¼″ × 10½″ | — |

# Make the Block

*Use the Tall Tree patterns (pullout page P2). For detailed instructions, refer to Key Technique: Foundation Paper Piecing (page 38).*

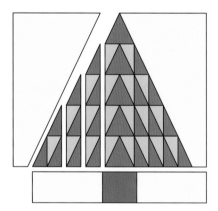

Tall Tree block assembly

**1.** Trace or photocopy Tall Tree foundation patterns A, B, C, D, E, F, G, H, and background pattern piece I.

**2.** Use the foundation paper piecing technique. Start with the center tree section A and begin at the bottom with triangle 1; continue in numerical order. Use a very short stitch length (1.0 mm or 24 stitches per inch) to perforate the paper, as this makes it much easier to remove later. Sew each of the remaining 6 tree branch sections and the trunk unit, being mindful of color placement.

**3.** Gently press the fabric side. Trim the sections, using the template paper as a guide.

**4.** Sew together the tree sections and carefully remove all the paper foundations.

**5.** Sew the 2 background triangles to the sides of the tree. Press the seams toward the background.

**6.** Sew the trunk unit to the bottom of the block and press the seam toward the trunk. Trim the block to 9″ × 9″.

**7.** Attach the side borders 1¼″ × 9″ and then the top and bottom borders 1¼″ × 10½″ to the block. Press the seams toward the borders.

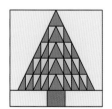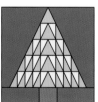

Tall Tree block alternate colorways

The last block to make for your quilter's primer is not technically a block at all. Yo-yos were a popular style of quiltmaking in the 1930s, when they were made of scraps of used clothing or feed, sugar, or flour sacks to make decorative coverlets. For today's quilter, they offer great design possibilities, a place to repurpose expensive fabric leftovers, and an easily portable project. This block finishes 5″ × 5″ and will be combined with the Zigzag block (page 37) and the Y and Z appliqué blocks (page 72) to create a 10″ × 10″ finished block.

## Materials

Choose 3 fabrics: 1 medium background, 1 dark, and 1 light.

Medium background: 5½″ × 5½″

Dark yo-yo: 9″ × 12″

Light yo-yo: 6″ × 6″

## Make the Block

*Use the Yo-Yo pattern (pullout page P2) to make a template. For detailed instructions on how to use patterns to make templates, refer to Key Technique: Make a Template (page 31).*

Yo-Yo block assembly

# YO-YO BLOCK

Yo-Yo block

**1.** Make a template using the Yo-Yo pattern.

**2.** Using the Yo-Yo template, trace and cut out 12 dark circles and 4 light circles. Do not add a seam allowance to the Yo-Yo template.

**3.** Using a double thickness of coordinating thread, hand sew a ¼″ hem with a running stitch around a circle. Leave long thread tails on both ends and do not knot.

**4.** With right sides out, gently pull up the thread tails (as a purse) until the center is quite tight. Sew a few final stitches to secure the yo-yo.

**5.** Flatten the yo-yo until it is a nice circle; then press.

**6.** Repeat Steps 3–5 to make 16 yo-yos.

**7.** Arrange the yo-yos with 4 lights in the center and 12 darks around the perimeter, as shown in the block assembly diagram. Sew together the yo-yos using a few blind stitches or whipstitches, as shown in Grandmother's Flower Garden Block, Step 5 photo (page 69).

**8.** Center the yo-yos on the background square. Tack down the centers and edges of all yo-yos with a few blind stitches. If you are making *The Quilter's Primer* with all your blocks, be sure to leave a good ¼″ seam allowance around the yo-yos, as they will be pieced with a Zigzag block.

Yo-Yo and Zigzag block assembly

## QUILTER'S PRIMER

*The Quilter's Primer* sampler quilt includes blocks with all the letters of the alphabet. Patterns are provided for a lovely hand-drawn alphabet that is very organic in appearance. Or choose a font on your computer and print out your own alphabet.

### Materials

Use scraps left over from earlier blocks to make the alphabet. Each letter uses two to four different fabrics, most of which are medium to medium-dark values. Choose just one fabric or a mix for the background pieces.

**Fabric for letters:** Approximately 1 yard total of medium and dark value scraps

**Fabric for background:** 2⅛ yards of 1 fabric (or use a mix)

### Cutting

For 26 blocks:

| FOR | CUT | SIZE |
|---|---|---|
| Background | 24 | 10½″ × 10½″ |
| | 2 | 5½″ × 5½″ |

*tip*

To prevent fraying, cut out just a few background blocks at a time rather than cutting all 26 at once.

## Make the Blocks

*Use the entire alphabet patterns (pullout pages P1–P2) to make templates. Note that letters C and G use the same pieces, as do letters E/F, O/Q, and P/R. For detailed instructions, refer to Key Technique: Make a Template (page 31) and Key Technique: Starch-Turned Appliqué (page 54).*

**1.** Trace the patterns required for the letter you are making onto the dull side of the heat-resistant plastic template material.

**2.** Prepare appliqué pieces following instructions for Starch-Turned Appliqué (page 54).

**3.** Arrange and center the appliqué pieces onto the background fabric in the shape of the letter you are making. As you work through the letters, it will become clear that some of the template pieces can be reused for more than one letter.

**4.** Appliqué the letter in place by hand or by machine.

# LOVE WALLHANGING

**FINISHED WALLHANGING: 25″ × 25″**

Pieced and quilted by Janet McWorkman

*This fun and easy wallhanging is a great wedding gift when made in the bride's colors. It morphs easily for other occasions too. Make it up in school colors to send off with your college student, use pastels for a baby's room, or go black, white, and gray for a very modern feel. Small projects like this are a great place to practice machine quilting skills.*

## Materials

Background: 4 squares 11″ × 11″

Appliqué letters: 12 scraps about 4″ × 10″

Inner border: ⅛ yard

Outer border: ⅜ yard

Binding: ⅜ yard

Backing: ⅞ yard

Batting: Crib size is plenty, or a 26″ × 26″ piece.

## Cutting

*WOF = width of fabric*

For 1 wallhanging:

| FOR | CUT | SIZE |
|---|---|---|
| Background squares | 4 | 10½″ × 10½″ |
| Inner border | 2 | 1″ × 20½″ |
| | 2 | 1″ × 21½″ |
| Outer border | 2 | 2½″ × 21½″ |
| | 2 | 2½″ × 25½″ |
| Letters | | Use templates. |
| Binding | 3 | 2¼″ × WOF |
| Backing | 1 | 26″ × 26″ |

## Make the Blocks

*Use the alphabet patterns for the letters L, O, V, and E (pullout page P1) to make templates. For detailed instructions, refer to Key Technique: Starch-Turned Appliqué (page 54).*

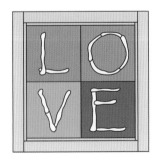

*LOVE wallhanging assembly*

**1.** Make the templates for the letters L, O, V, and E.

**2.** Turn under the ¼″ seam allowances on each piece.

**3.** Glue and sew the letters to the background squares.

**4.** Sew together the 4 blocks.

**5.** Sew the 2 inner border strips 1″ × 20½″ to the top and bottom. Sew the 2 border strips 1″ × 21½″ to the sides. Press all the seams toward the border pieces.

**6.** Repeat Step 5 with the outer border pieces.

## Finish the Wallhanging

*For detailed instructions on making a quilt sandwich, quilting, and binding, refer to Quiltmaking Basics (page 13).*

### Sandwich, Quilt, and Bind

**1.** Make a quilt sandwich with the backing, batting, and top.

**2.** Quilt, using the method of your choice.

**3.** Bind the wallhanging.

**4.** Label and love.

# FINISHING YOUR PRIMER

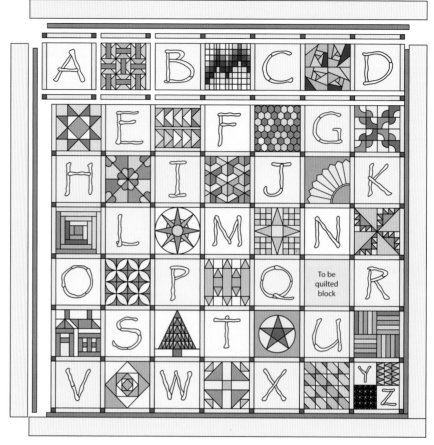

*The Quilter's Primer* quilt assembly

You've come to that wonderful place where all the primer blocks are pieced and appliquéd. Congratulations!

Here's a quilt assembly diagram of *The Quilter's Primer*. Note that there are seven blocks across the top and seven blocks down the sides. Between each block is a sashing strip. Where these strips meet, there are small squares, called *cornerstones*. The quilt has a thin inner border and a wider outer border.

## Materials

*This list assumes that you already have completed all the blocks for the quilt top, with the exception of the "To be quilted block." This block is an opportunity to showcase quilting that is perhaps different form the body of the quilt. It is not a pieced block; rather it is a blank slate for the quilter. The background piece is treated like a pieced block. You can elect to hand quilt just this one block and machine quilt the rest. Or, if you are sending out your quilt to be professionally quilted, this one block can be addressed as a space to showcase a quilting design of your choosing.*

Background: 11″ × 11″
(for quilted block)

Sashing: 1½ yards

Cornerstones: ¼ yard

Inner border: ½ yard

Outer border: 1½ yards

Binding: 1 yard

Backing: 7¾ yards

Batting: King-size (92″ × 92″)

## Cutting

*WOF = width of fabric*

| FOR | CUT | SIZE |
|---|---|---|
| Background | 1 | 10½″ × 10½″ |
| Sashing | 112 | 1½″ × 10½″ |
| Cornerstones | 64 | 1½″ × 1½″ |
| Inner border | 8 | 1½″ × WOF |
| Outer border | 9 | 4½″ × WOF |
| Binding | 10 | 2¼″ × WOF |

# Finish the Quilt Top

*For detailed instructions, refer to Quiltmaking Basics (page 13).*

Arrange all the blocks as shown in *The Quilter's Primer* assembly diagram (previous page).

## Sashing and Cornerstones

**1.** Sew sashing strips to the left side of each block. Sew sashing strips to the right side of the 7 blocks in the far right column.

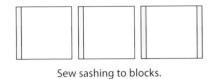

Sew sashing to blocks.

**2.** Sew the 7 rows of blocks, being careful of block placement. Press the seam allowances toward the sashing strips.

**3.** Sew the 7 sashing strips between 8 cornerstones as shown. Press the seam allowances toward the sashing strips.

Alternate cornerstones and sashing.

**4.** Refer to the quilt assembly diagram and sew the Step 3 strips to the rows of blocks, carefully matching the cornerstone seams to the vertical sashing strips. Press the seams toward the sashing strips.

## Add Borders

**1.** Sew all the inner border strips end to end. Cut the long strip into 2 pieces each 1½″ × 78½″ and attach them to the sides of the quilt top. Cut the remaining long strip into 2 pieces each 1½″ × 80½″ and attach these to the top and bottom of the quilt. Press the seams toward the borders.

**2.** Sew together all the outer border pieces end to end. Cut the long strip into 2 pieces each 4½″ × 80½″ and attach them to the sides of the quilt top. Cut 2 pieces each 4½″ × 88½″ and attach to the top and bottom of the quilt. Press the seams toward the borders.

**3.** Sew a scant ¼″ around the entire perimeter of the quilt to give it stability during the quilting process.

# Finish the Quilt

*For detailed instructions on making a quilt sandwich, quilting, and binding, refer to Quiltmaking Basics (page 13).*

## Backing

**1.** Cut 2 pieces of backing fabric 94″ × WOF and 1 piece 32″ × WOF. Cut the 32″ piece into 3 strips 13″ × 32″.

**2.** Refer to the backing layout diagram and sew the center pieces together; then add the outer rectangles. Press the seams open.

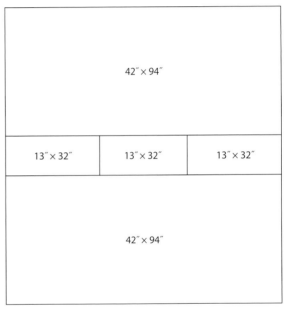

Backing layout

## Sandwich, Quilt, and Bind

**1.** Make a quilt sandwich with the backing, batting, and top.

**2.** Quilt, using the method of your choice.

**3.** Bind the quilt.

**4.** Label and love.

# TIPS AND TRICKS

## AT THE MACHINE

- Write your normal sewing machine settings on a sticky note and keep it with your supplies. It will be invaluable after you change the settings for special-purpose sewing.

- If your foot pedal tends to slide out of range, attach a strip of sticky-back hook-and-loop tape (the loopy side) to the bottom.

## FABRIC CARE

- Perform a burn test if you're unsure whether a piece of fabric is 100 percent cotton. Cotton will burn to ash. Polyester will curl and melt.

- When prewashing fabric, open the piece completely to prevent setting in the fold line.

- Snip the corners of new fabric before prewashing and drying. It will reduce raveling, and you'll know instantly if it has been preshrunk when you pull it out of your stash years later.

## IRONING

- Make friends with good-quality spray starch and keep some nearby. Use it to give body to very thin fabrics prior to cutting, to finish off a quilt block prior to squaring-up, and to flatten out stubborn creases.

- Use rubbing alcohol to remove fusible web residue from your cold iron.

- With your iron set to the hot setting, press used dryer sheets to make your iron glide easier.

- Irons can be very finicky, rusting up and spitting rusty water. Always empty the iron of all water and store it upside down. Or, never use the steam feature; use a spray water bottle instead.

## CUTTING

- Raise your cutting table and save your back—use a set of four inexpensive table lifts, available at home improvement stores.

- Keep an empty rotary blade case marked "used" to store old blades for safe recycling.

- Clean your cutting mat with a dry plastic pot scrubber.

- Keep your cutting mats out of direct sunlight, as they may warp.

## TOOLS

- Always label your tools. They have an uncanny ability to walk away of their own volition but seem to stay home if they have a label.

- Use a large, felt-backed, vinyl tablecloth as an inexpensive (and space saving) alternative to building a design wall. Arrange your quilt on the felt side and roll it up for safe keeping. Your blocks will stay right where you put them. Nifty!

- Use empty pill bottles to hold broken or bent needles for safe disposal.

- Use a small Phillips screwdriver to turn corners right side out.

- Use the color chips at paint centers as design tools when playing with color.

## AND REMEMBER

- Keep a tube of superglue in your sewing box. If you cut yourself or prick a finger while working on a project, a drop of glue will prevent you from bleeding all over your fabric.

- Label a gift quilt with your name and the date it was made. Also, include washing and drying instructions.

- If your collection of fabric starts to grow into an unwieldy stash, consider donating fabric to your local senior center.

- Rather than tossing small scraps of fabric away, cut them into usable squares and strips stored in plastic containers. Before you know it, you'll have plenty to make a scrap quilt, which will also be a testament to all the prior quilts you've made.

- Consider joining a local quilt guild. They are people of like mind and inspiration—and they always know where good sales are found.

**SUNFLOWERS AROUND THE COURTHOUSE**, 69″ × 79″,
Pattern by Judy Fojut, pieced by Janet McWorkman,
quilted by Laurie Vandergriff

**CIVIL WAR SPARKLE**, 72″ × 72″,
Pattern by Marilyn Doheny, pieced by Janet McWorkman,
quilted by Laurie Vandergriff

**RED POPPIES ON YELLOW**, 84″ × 84″,
Pieced by Janet McWorkman, quilted by Laurie Vandergriff

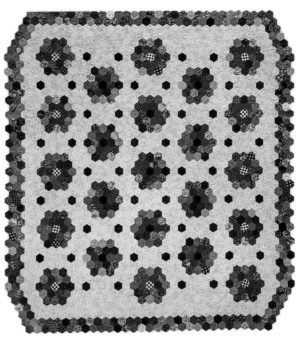

**GRANDMOTHER'S HOLIDAY FLOWERS**, 72″ × 84″,
Pieced and hand quilted by Janet McWorkman

**SANTA'S MUKLUK**, 24″ × 32″,
Pieced and quilted by Janet McWorkman

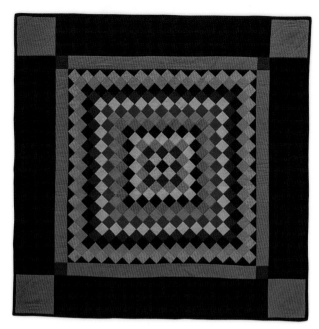

**AMISH SUNSHINE AND SHADOW**, 46″ × 46″,
Pieced and quilted by Lisa Bauer

**DON'S MARINER'S COMPASS**, 57″ × 57″,
Pattern by Brenda Henning,
pieced and quilted by Janet McWorkman

**PASTORAL STARS**, 40″ × 68″,
Pieced and quilted by Kathleen Richards and Grace Matsutani